$25.00

COLLECTED POETRY

COLLECTED POETRY

LOUIS DUDEK

DELTA CANADA

Published by Delta Canada, 5 Ingleside Avenue,
Montreal 215, Canada.

ISBN 0-919162-31-2

CONTENTS

1. EARLY POEMS

2. LYRICS & IMAGES

3. MEDITATION OVER A WINTRY CITY

6. POETRY AND TRUTH

7. PURE SCIENCE

8. LAUGHING STALKS

9. EN MEXICO

10. SELECTIONS FROM ATLANTIS

Prologue (entire)
Part I, Section 1 (in part)
Part II, Section 1 (in part)
Part II, Section 3 (entire)
Part III, Section 2 (entire)
Part III, Section 3 (entire)
Epilogue (entire)

11. JEUX & DIVERTISSEMENTS

Alba
Erotic Tropes
Les Répétitions
The Process
Fictions, Supreme or Otherwise
Confidential
Sad Thoughts
But Aren't All Poets Poets' Poets?
From the Chinese
Brightness
Fragments 1
Fragments 2
Ice Cream

12. REFLECTIONS AFTER ATLANTIS

The Demolitions
Canada: Interim Report
A Circle Tour of the Rockies
Continuation I

1:

EARLY POEMS

IMPROVISATION

Inhaling the air, a boy on a tricycle,
a child, holding the sleeves of passers-by,
and on the sidewalk a kitten
nestling and curling,
that an old man tosses and teases;
a slender girl lying on the grass
soft, on her stomach,
the arches of her feet bowed out . . .

I rest my eyes on the horizon
still on the warm ground,
following a streetcar down a hillside
sliding on the street like jelly;
or a girl
whose hips glide to and fro
on ball-bearings and globes of her body
with the prostitute face, spent, indifferent;
or in vertigoes of the sky
saying, "Grab the sun,
it won't stay long . . . not long . . ."

The fellow at the gate who mumbles,
the girl at the counter stiffened like a tree
pass into eyes that are sensitive to the sun;
I rise in elevators where the derricks run
and trail on the prairies,
seeing grain stores stand like thirsting men;
machinery on Charlie Chaplin feet
speeds, and sticks, and comes to a halt
and speeds again.

Like electricity that darts and ceases,
my eyes filling my eyelids
trace a face seen only on misted mornings
or in vertigoes of star-swept skies;
and in the midst of these, secret as any,
they move and move in the quick atmosphere.

SOUND FOR ORCHESTRA

The shined bugle of my ear
can hear the night-hawk muffle a torch
somewhere welding a wheel-way, and the purr
of mounted-on-rubber wagons
under a bridge, hold off a whistle.

I heard an echo from the heavy hills
like a wind on a wave, where the girl stood
by a fence post, listening,
her hills empty of rovers
or lovers, her lips open and dry.
The air came warm in the long afternoon,
and she called, but caught only echoes,
which under an arch I caught, too.
I spoke, and the sound fell
like a ball on a wall, or a word in a well.

Then, the boy, wondering,
open-legged, not knowing
why he was somewhat held, or freed
to move and perhaps collapse
on the ice. What I heard was the singing
of the frozen ice-sheet, in the boy's mountain,
and the high note he made like a tiger.

O the marimba, the cackling cornet
on a sudden, in the streets,
jazzing the brain's liquors,
melting the mountains and laying down the hills—
these props for tomorrow's waste!
The stops break and the wind breaks—
you bring the boy and the girl together, and the kazoo.
But the ecstasy will finish fast as sex;
they will sit building
hills and mountains like a diastrophism.

While the creaking, four-legged chair of the bachelor
contented on Sunday strokes out its sound,
he sits clean-collared, in tranquil isolation,
unneedful of needles, his work done,
and the notes play a violin sonata,
andantino, extending an afternoon.

These sang the music of occupations, still sing;
but to the last, my ear's bugle turned
wanting sounds like brass keys
that would open a symphony's doors.
None came. Alone, I listen at night
to sounds from the river like a funneled horn.

NIGHT SCENE

I meant to be walking in the night-time,
But I lean here, for the street is quiet.
It is very still between the buildings.
No one passes.
Somewhere I hear the notes of a piano,
And into my head drift the words of a poem
Which a while ago I was reading.
I notice how the light from a window
Falls upon the snow in the alley;
The street is quite deserted.
Now a man passes,
Making no more sound than a shadow.
Above me a few stars quietly
Stay between the dark houses.

AT PARTING

Know, that as a rose unpetals in the morning
So your lips unpetal under my lips;

And also, like a bird sleeping with wings folded,
Your eyelids sleep under my kisses.

But like a road running through cornfields
Is the length of your arm when you are saying good-bye;

And like a city crumbling, in ruin,
Is my emotion when the door closes.

Like a streetcar, like a terrible tractor,
It is all rumbling and tumbling in me when you are gone.

YORICK

Twin cones are scooped in skull bones
Where once eyes were, and no thing now presses
Upon the inside of this dome, the mosaic of it
Is well fitted, but an ant dances
On the dais.

Clipped, the winged withers cannot
Lift him, eating air,
The ventilation, one way, two way,
Plays through his toothless jaw.

Aerodrome ribs grace ether,
Caterpillar spine crawls to burrow,
O how a beetle dines
Upon a pelvic plateful
Of his marrow.

Binoculars for backside, how he sprawls.
The awkward
Collapse of two-pronged legs would make
You philosophers howl.

A FACTORY ON SUNDAY

That yellow chimney up against the sky,
Black up one funnel to the top,
Is a tower built for a strange god,
With watches at the turrets stationed
To guard over the fires of their lord.

But it is also the bossed bludgeon
Of the ape-man and barbarian:
A symbol of his lust for power
Set in the ground to stand
In the sight of the cowed and beaten.

Then, most of all, it has the mystery
Of an occult Egyptian censer
Held in the hands of priests,
Sending incense down to the people,
Making them bow down and pray.

THE SEA

I

Ghostlike against the sun
You stand, and scan
A track upon the flood,
Glistering, gone.

Your thin arm raised
To the bright sea
Is knife-like against
Reality;

And warm, lost man,
Like solar light
You make globed worlds,
And dread the night;

Or think of sped time
Run like a glass,
Where the bright road
Vanishes,

For each ray mirrors
A split past,
And fiction disappears
In plain glass.

II

From change to still memory
Water widens,
And in its breathless air
No man hides;

Distinct in white sun
With rooks and towers,
Peopled and green, flee
The far shores.

Adrift in the fast flood
Of present light,
There is no shade from final
Sun's sight:

All vision in the eyes
Of love gone
Is hurt by the quick, material
Glance of sun;

And maidens with spun hair
And lips red
Bleed like a blood weed
Their thin blood.

Think of a pale girl
You once loved,
And held by a small wrist
Imprisoned . . .

Your once caught vision
Of white linen
Wet with her tears like rain,
Abandon:

A dream of cosmic accident
Lost in living,
Sweet fruit that night frost
Nipped for evil.

Seek for new ilots
Of hurt desire,
Where shed sunlight prances
A fresh fire.

If there is bitter truth
To taste and swallow,
Know that the same gruel
Is medicine and food.

Though men may live like Job
In a long sorrow,
Crying that the great gods
Are cruel,

Death itself is curable
In the human body,
Though one generation find
No near recovery.

III

O hear the voice of the wind!
The sun is down,
He splays the waves where your bright
Visions drown!

Hear the night wind
On a spumed sea,
How he gathers the scud and breaks
It menacingly.

In the dark, whirling wave
Is a green home,
Quiet and secret anchor
For tired bone . . .

Though wink the sunny islands
Eyes have seen,
They will vanish in mirage,
Sharp and keen,

And foot will feel no shores
That man found
Mirrored in glassy ikons
Of the mind;

But like thin, springtime edges
Of ice in sea
Will vanish where long grass
Waves silently,

Where on the floor of oceans,
Tiered and reefed,
Rise in flower and in coral
Cities in the deep.

There, drifted at last, hands
Moveless fold,
And eyes the liquid limes
Lave and remold

To keep there for ageless
Time entombed,
The chemistry of flesh
Sealed and fused;

Till barebacked, whole, and hard,
Rending the deep,
Leviathan continents shall rise
Where oceans sleep,

And portals your lime and clay
Shall open apart,
In cities high with wonder
Of heroic art . . .

O for these, the cities,
(Hear the wind!)
Shall the fire of your bones
Be cold, be stilled.

2:

LYRICS & IMAGES

MAKING POEMS

Hanging over a rail of the harbour bridge,
knocking mud
out of the corners and angles of shoes,
diverting traffic
I am walking full of poems; I make them
hitting home runs, taking the sun,
worrying, looking at people.
I am breathing under the excitement.

ROMANTIC LYRIC

The cloth-white ferns on these winter windows
remind me of Monday mornings, and frozen washing
and billows of bubbling steam
which would be rising from the doorways: I remember it all,
as I stand at this window and watch the wind blow.

O, but the weather's changed! I see the wind more
than the ferns, and I am more cold than I was then.
I do not love the warmth indoors either;
no more, waiting thin before the window
while there, a white thing
something I have imagined and loved
falls like a cold fluttering bird.

EVENING

The noise of these buildings
quietens down.
The rage of these busy streets
dies down and becomes still.
The hardness
softens, and is forgotten
when the lamps fade
and silently the dark gathers
on the walls.

NIGHT PIECE

The moon floated down
a river between two clouds,
melted the stone banks and they
were gone.
Never flew the stars
in pebbles so brilliant,
nor shook the sands
in such sediments!

A PARK

Between the trees in the park
the light falls like rain
and flows into pools of gold.

People in the distance
like dim figures on a screen
or ghosts, in thin watery outline.

But near, in front of the sun,
there are men, solid and strong,
moulded in black iron.

There, is that other world,
of fiction, where we used to live
yesterday, before we suffered;
but here is where we have come through,
are men, moulded to pillars of stone.

LATE WINTER

The sky is scrubbed clean,
        the chimneys stand like springtime sticks
growing out into a world done over.
A fresh lacquer of rain
        dries on the tree branches.

        But the sun is stony
on the houses, on walls of factory metal,
on the tops of buildings
        distinct as in a mortuary.
On the distant roofs it lies cold
like platinum, that the waste
        cotton clouds have polished.
Nature stiffens
        her water-tints in times like these,
makes morals out of her fairy-tales.

MAY

Already in May
the relaxed legs of summer
that girls have,

the dog
on his flying trapeze
by the tall hedge,

public yet peaceable,
while a stiff robin
hops on the hard green.

Well, I remember—
watching the birds nesting in cracked walls—
how the sparrows twittered in our skylight

one shrilly spring
when I was a long
skinny boy;

it was good
for my clean curiosity,
and my melodious intelligence

listened to it . . . But look,
a cloud in the shape of a unicorn,
and those buds, bursting in the branches!

NOON

Along the piers and by the dockyards,
Like a weird cloud, or a ghost in a cathedral,
Floating, I go towards the freight-cars
And the railings, feeling the brittle sun:
But I become a shrill cloud seen at noontime
Under the sharp silk shot from the sun.

I had imagined that maggots had eaten me
And abandoned my bones to the cheerless air,
I had thought that death had made me a stone
Dull to the sun, and to the life it sprinkles . . .

But now the sun wields his ax from a scabbard
And splits the sidewalk like a slab of steel;
The glass of the buildings that he has shattered
Falls ringing on the square, on the heads of people.

MIDSUMMER, ADIRONDACKS

Somewhere in the Adirondack gold
of buttercups and purple clover, slumbering
but brilliant blood strawberries run by the road,
run when you lift the leaves and wake them,
from the sun-suffering and slain hills
and the white blades of heat;
          and they hide in the shades,
lovely and strong by the mountainsides,
by the rocks, the roads, and the woolly trees.

And there the anger of every river
like a mad mountain Michaelangelo carves
castles and caves in the green stones,

and glad with its message thunders
down from the mountains, waving maniac white hair
like a beautiful man.

There in the hills, we kissed.
In the streams, pebble-naked
—your body bread-brown, then shining,
        shining with drops, bewildered with water—
your kisses bright as those berries I had,
kissed your lips like a rock, with mad water kisses.

SKYSCRAPER WINDOW

At the ice-bright window,
if you let the light
dazzle you with silver blisters from
the hump-backed cars, that crawl
aching, in rows
to a green light,
and if you look
down canyons, into distant boroughs
where at last they die like proboscidians
among the ivories and striated marbles
of St. James street,
you may wonder if history
ever knew, or would have been surprised;
if in the streets, the cries
and the coughing in corners,
and the falcons fluttering with blood-stained beaks
could have been foretold
for our pity and amazement,
and whether the nerves we learn by,
teeth, and veins, are tough enough,
and weaponed
to break alive into the green beyond.

WOMAN

These are poetry, which would be sung—
the budding genitals, the fearful phallus,
man's elemental organs as beautiful
as a geyser rising suddenly upward,
a wonder woman will always love.
Stroking the foam of violent hair
and bathing under the soft spray
beating up from masculine marble,
the virgin will become brown and ripe
her body radiating with the sun.
At her touch some irrepressible lad
like an eaglet under a dove's wing
will thresh with menace, and assault
her fears with infinite excitement.
Secret genitals—wonders to be sung!
And woman, if she support the storm
of that chaotic ocean rolling over
her world shattered by male strength,
if tasting the bowels of the earth
in their salt, malignant purity,
she return to love, and to man's cruelty
her whip of nature, asleep and weak—
her reward is to walk with sun-born women,
such as own the skies, and mother great birds.

THE BEE OF WORDS

Her mouth opening in lovely speech is the wet leaf
of a flower, her voice the bee's soft sound in the air
bringing the sting of desire; under the light of her hair
the bee of words runs and robs like a loaded thief.

I am the hot hive to which those bee words come,
my palace floors swept clean for their sultry wings;
out of the light into my dark cave each one brings
its sweetness that it stores in the mind's honeycomb.

There, of that clear honey, love like a queen bee wives
in dark fertility; and of her honeyed streams
unborn bees will rise up in their cells from dreams
of a myriad shining wings whirled out to a million hives.

What generation of smoke turning to golden clouds
does love make of a warm mouth and its own burning?
What lands of love, for which those waxen wings are yearning,
will yield them honeyed fields and apples breaking the boughs?

IN SPRING

In spring, the air is magnetic,
wherever girls and boys meet
the eyes are north and south poles
oscillating in unison.

In spring the young are especially graceful—
six-year-olds tumble like sweet potatoes,
boys of eight get rapacious,
girls go dreamy.

And the wreck of fire-escapes seems blacker
in the shining morning;
and the black bean of the sick, shaven slum child
in the iron seems entangled.

Yet love insists on being important:
youth and sweet sixteen lean on the doorpost
at evening—
Clark Gable and Lana Turner.

The stars melt like snowdrops.
A warm wind erases
the rising vapour of the city from view,
and even the refuse in the streets
looks romantic.

NIGHT TRAIN

The heads of these people—baggage—paper—fur—
And the great flares of matches lighted in the train.
                                        Outside, smoke crossing the country
Fretted with oil tanks and forgotten freight cars,
                                                            then the river
Frozen under the bridge, whose banging black girders
Break across the snow-swept shrubbery
                                                of the river shallows;
Then the singing wires of telegraphs
And the silent fences
                at the beginnings and endings of forests.
A milky emulsion of sky—the motion
Of the railroad's belly pounding under us—
While within the lighted car, in the loudness,
Girls sit, their heads bowed over books,
Ferreting the pages of love, unsatisfied.

AT THE ROUND WINDOW

Between the apartment's glass glittering windows,
in the jungle of a tree,
arrested time with a fluttering of the branches
rests unchangeable in our protean age—
like silence cupped in a human hand.
And at the tree's feet
the sparrows brush the pathway
with wings a blaze of action:
old as a wave on a stone, they break with panic life.
And they have hopped since the first and earliest bird,
and cell-like move in an infinite wide pattern
in the microscopic wafer of a slide,
while we build a changing sky of glass.
Does there beat in the breast of every bird
the same novelty and discovery,
as if he, the first bird, and only true bird,
breathed this life, found this leaf?

TREE IN A STREET

Why will not that tree adapt itself to our tempo?
We have lopped off several branches,
cut her skin to the white bone,
run wires through her body and her loins,
yet she will not change.
Ignorant of traffic, of dynamos and steel,
as uncontemporary
as bloomers and bustles
she stands there like a green cliché.

CLOUDS

Pale from the storm's mouth
the white clouds move out,
they slowly turn
like hills of clouded ice
or winter glass before our eyes.
Under their shadows burn
battered buildings ashamed,
tenements under East River
under a project of new homes;
the flapping fringes of the city
cower and cover their knees and bones.
But the clouds are not sad
on this account. Can it be that,
somewhere, they see beyond
mountains and green lands?
They move like the Greek philosophers,
wreathed in smiles,
as if the knowledge of love
and timeless peace made them mild.

ON POETRY

The flame of a man's imagination should be organic with his body,
coincident with an act, like an igniting spark.
But mostly, he fails in the act
and expels his bad humour in visions. A man curses,
seeing the thing he hates in pain, cursed by his vision:
this is poetry, action unrealized:
what we want most we imagine most, like self-abusing boys.

Lately, of woman man has been deprived
—the smaller man and the greater too—
and in all the language of his verse
love, love, love
he cries, never having enough.

Formerly, it was different.
Hairy and sensible, he needed food
when he painted steak chops (bison meat)
in a gaping cave; a bird, or juicy calves of mammoth,
his midday meals.
He carved these also on his spears
and on the handles of knives,
handing the art down the generations.

But with the coming of civilization
his body desired other food at times, less personal,
but unattainable. So the poet, who had vision,
wanted to be capable of commanding God, like Jeremiah;
but denied, he ranted poetry.

The poet should have been a king,
Shakespeare should have been all his monarchs, ruling England,
Homer should have been Achilles
frowning for Briseis, or fighting for his friend.
These great ones imagined grandly,
the life of the body having defaulted.

So in our time the poet,
in need of quiet, order in chaos,
complete community, wants something he does not have
in all nakedness. And so he wrestles
with the maiden, his wild dream, in his sleep.

3: MEDITATION OVER A WINTRY CITY

MEDITATION OVER A WINTRY CITY

What vast raft of brick and black
iron hanging
by ropes of smoke from the blue winter
stands on the snows of the country?
What city, spreading like tar, of streets and people?

Among the pewters
on steps and alley pails, on red streaks
of streets, against black doors—
viewless as fleas,
profuse as bacilli or as tiny beetles
crawling around stones, wingless,
swift-footed, traceless, silent—
move points, populations, people!
A wonder, a paradox, a thing for laughter . . .
How such diminutive countless men have glued
splinter on splinter, web on web,
the world that hives them. A creation of flies.

Round about, the earth is ice-cold, the sky steely.
In holes of refuse heaped mountain-high
skyward, steamed in odor and comfort,
multiplying and eating,
the creative animal, inventor of the nail
and the screwdriver, nests and sleeps,
counts the slow hours of winter, breathes
like a blind fish in warm water:
who, naked, would have frozen stiff as flannels,
would have turned over like a poisoned insect!
Not three of him would have outlived this cold.
A cold planet.

To live. To breathe the crystal air
yet a while longer. To hold this shape and motion
and precarious mind unbroken. Not to die.
To live in the seed, to put forth a child.
To continue. To hold anxiously

to the crumbling earth, and swim
still in the sea of air and light. Not to die.
To leave a sign. To mark a stone with a name.
To leave a house with a deed. To make a cross.
To die undyingly. To say the word
that echoes through time:
to make the stars hear.

And yet, bloated buildings, and citadels of stone,
and jewelry of light as night comes on,
castles among hovels, parks, facades, driveways,
tell one of something harder than bread
that men will work for, more than life merely,
fearless of death.
Strange, that a feeble animal
marked for extinction and beset with the seasons,
with cold, and lack,
and danger from the invisible unknown dark,
should lust
to overpower or out-possess his kind,
his tiny double, helpless kin;
should bite and pinch, and slaughter,
to extirpate his like;
should live richer than another, in a bigger box,
and starve his own poor kind—and of this be proud.
If men are not equal it is the curse of pride,
not of necessity. One is rich
only where others are poor. It is not for goods themselves
but for the difference with what others have
that stones are piled and power shows its face
as in a mirror in every street.
But man is ignorant as a falling stone,
ignorant as water, or as fire,
moved by a passion and a blind instinct
to these fanatic motions.
Were he sure and wise
as the seed that grows, godlike in the knowledge
into what plant or flower it grows! . . .
Wise he once was, perhaps; but since that time
having eaten strange fruit he goes

drunk with wild passions, in crooked ways,
an enemy to strangers, unkind to his own kin,
while the cold winds of death blow down on him,
and women wail and old men weep for shame.

How can this bring him good? The harm is done.
All ignorance is evil, since each step taken
by man, the intellectual god, is a dreadful choice
and a responsibility that cuts him off
from natural things, which have no choice,
from stones, and streams, and sunset winds.
His every footstep in the tracks
that turn and tie about his feet,
stumbling like a blind man going home,
unguided by the light of an extending mind, may touch
the precipice of this world, and then he falls
headlong, revolving among trees and stones,
stricken, a poor and wounded thing.

And yet there is a glorious logic and a god
in every force that moves a life,
a leaf opening to the sun, a bird his wings,
or a man's hand.
None is least, and all are one
with that which moves the stars, which neither cruelly
nor in kindness, but with painful effort
has come to breathe in a living thing.
It is by that force men move,
the reason only free to make adjustments
subtler than those a bee or a blossom makes.
The wise know this.
So the word of the wise is angry, it is against this world,
though in its nature helpless almost, like a lifted hand
against a gun. Its work is slow.
It builds, not homes, but cities made of words:
cities within our cities, mining from within.
The wise may draw what often cannot be
built at all; or if it can be, is ignored.
Insulted by the ear that waits for facts,
set aside by active men,

stalked by disease and death, as all men are,
drowned in the apparent chaos of these times,
artists and scholars walk their quiet ways,
echo the pain that other men should feel, and understand,
and make their voices heard as something seen, above all sound.

I have made loud the disarray
of my own mind. A comet is not more wild
than the lights of this city shining at my feet.
In the great darkness, the commotions of that life
rise like the shoutings of applause: there man is strong and proud.
A poet must be weak before so great a thing.
Who can move the stars? And is man less than a star?
More bright, more flagrant, in this place where now I stand.
And where is the centre, at which God stands?
It is where I stand. But now it snows.
No, the snow cannot put out those lights;
and would not. It falls as quietly
as old poetry on the stones of the city,
on the roofs and the staircases, and the walking people;
it falls, making them suddenly white as flowers.

EAST OF THE CITY

East of the city, under towering smokestacks
Where the railroad, brewery and tall bridge
Redden and drown our eyes with cinders,
Where the drumhead oilskin of the river wavers,
And in the damp the steam's hiss tells how earnest
Industry's effort is, as it impersonalizes
And soon hisses you out of the way:
Between the knees of the bridge, crouching
By a wall that gapes like a stupid face—
Pause, and see how heavy the corpses
Swing from the girders, how their shadows resound
As they shudder and fall from the beams.

Out of the ruptured cauldron, the green factory
Whose ogre eyes gleam in the sooty night,
Railed wrists stretch over hard, broad hills,
The cold coal and straight strata, iron and steel;
The belly boils, and peal its shattering bells
Of hammers and cranes, flying their halleluyas.

Where in a crimson doorway like a sour red rind—
A round of citrus sucked in the mouth—
The haggard labourers gather, muster together;
Dwarfed by the dark, they shrink in showers
Of light spat from the walls by the welders,
Then club-footed, hunched, they shoulder through
A cloud of golden atoms, shredded fireworks.

They sling their thumbs through their lax suspenders
On rags of shirt crossing their barren shoulders,
Wipe the wrinkles round their throats and ear-lobes,
And plod the streets together; or sometimes rowdying
Like fresh bloodhounds bound and menace peace—
While behind them trail the thin, coughing fathers,
And perhaps a few girls draped in dirty aprons.

A rumble in a saloon, the guttural boom of voices—
Headlong through smoke and laughter—the giggle of gargoyles—
Hectic veins that stand blue and clear of the skin
At the magnified wafers, tables like eucharists!
Troughfuls of cloggy sawdust float on the floor,
And on the dim walls, weak with hallucined females,
Great teats under veils, the secrets seen,
Sit bathers and nymphs, displayed for the toothless
Who would lie there and saunter, feel the breasts fertile.

Ah, here over their lager, thick and throaty,
Maudlin with pleasure, or sucking strong cigars,
They turn in phalanx against their bosses
Like impotent rats in cages, or gnawing at curtains.
Free with their money, knocking the metal on tables,
Their eyes boast of terrible strength, and wrestle
With tree roots, in the thunder of their imaginations:
They handle rough nuggets that might buy them freedom,
But lose them in the loam of prejudice, tired and ignorant.

Then late, on stairs like a broken accordion
They mount to the two-room flat, smelling a cloth
That wraps their faces and tangles at their feet;
They eat the cold supper, leaning on their elbows
And grousing, while the wife tense in the kitchen
Waits with lukewarm water, and the fecal dishes.
Afterwards, leaning limp out of windows
They look at life in the street, wait for bedtime;
Then dark comes, and the white, silent patches
Of their faces, grow dim and disappear in the houses.

See, the makers of wheels heave their heavy hammers
With hands they spit on and slap to leather aprons
Tough as their skins. Their feet on the concrete floor
Hold the lead levers of their solid bodies;
Their shoulders are walls for work; their eyes
Rich with the rolling light of torches,
The flames of an armoury where a world is welded.

The wheel is hoisted on a crane; the builders are proud
And powerful, and know without book how to heave it.
They draw together in strength, bronze carven figures
Who lift the iron on beams, and roll it sideways
With cleavers—and loud, shivering the soul,
They ram down clamps of iron, rivets into steel.

No clever gill in an office nor salaried executive,
Nor any who stands by with blueprint and paper
Knows these tools, or the hard skill it takes.
But look, how forceful with facts, the sullen slaves
Here powerful and proud, stand up as leaders.
No thread runs in the rounded wheel without them.
The wheel of society, steel-bright with the future,
Is wrought by the people, its only revolutionists.
See, how the war clouds boil around the factories—
For here at last will break, brilliantly, scrolled in the stars,
The searing bolts of cloud-biting thunder!

So that someday we may go, and see the sun rise
Outside this world of rubble. Drive out
Through factories, and brick walls of buildings,
To the east, to the fields sweet with clover
Where over the heads of trees, in a cup of the sky,
Laughing, the earth-warmer comes, making day warm for us,
A world white with morning, white with sunlight!
For this, take up a handful of green grass for hope:
Walk out tomorrow, talk to the world and people.

UPSTATE TOURISM

Upstate in New York
they hang rambling roses on their porches,
blankets and red rugs of them;
farther, streets of red strawberries will greet you,
hills of apples, plums, grapes, cherries
in speckled orchards
(though the brown fields lie fallow,
famous for their rocks),
and you will be aware of daisies
blowing across the fields, and the smell of clover
and buttercups, cricket sounds in the air,
and waves of shadow that the white clouds make
running over the round hills.

But if one is struck amid the generosity of nature
by the growing insanity apparent in the villages,
rust around the canneries, and the shambles the Joads left,
old pails, and lean-to outhouses,
or by the factory
exploding its whistle into the country air
(the town side-streets falling away
with a clatter of ash-cans
like the tail on a 'Just Married' car;
and the doorsteps crumbling where
mysteriously sits a ragged generation—
bits of flesh torn from their fathers, chewing hands),
there is still an elm somewhere against the clouds,
a distant barn, or a steeple
hard as a stone against the sky, to look at;
they will meet the tourist's eyes with promise of plenty,
cooled by the cold wind
or the evidence of rust on the broken tools of survival.

OLD CITY SECTOR

This gut-end of a hungry city
costive with rock and curling ornament,
once glorious, the pride of bankers,
reaches each projecting cornice
over the stomach of empty air, the street
now deserted.

Here every morning an old rich idiot
in a worn, shining suit stumbles,
ignoring the soft sun, and the imaginary note
of the chanticleer somewhere singing—
taps his stick on the green-gold morning door,
then turns the lock with a big key, opens and enters;
he boards the ugly small safe in the corner
and on his knees, peels out the dusty dollars—
the sun on his desk shaking, a pool dripping with mermaids.

Later, enter the pinched clerks and the typists,
hating the grime that gathers on the sills
and the soot that slides from the chimneys;
they work and wait for their simple Sundays,
for the evening show, or sex,
always in the grip and tension of this intestine,
the small capitalist's greedy space
of warehouse and foetid factory
where tight-fisted profit is squeezed out
in the torsions of crass inequity and private bitterness.

LOOKING AT STENOGRAPHERS

Product of the dactylo, they are like their stamped paper,
the keys cover their eyes and brains.
Should an idea suddenly appear
like a snakehead, they are hilarious and panicky,
though God is behind the curtain of their inane stage:
religion not to be assaulted; so they jive with God in their arms.
Society their cage, in which they sit etherized and serve,
has no existence for their pale universe; and even sex
scarcely interposes between the sheets,
although they chatter about dreams
occasionally *flying* and *rapier thrusts*
but usually wish limousines, small jealousies or sweet foods.
So, superficially shingled with editorial words, gleanings
        from the magazines,
tomorrow they will drink tea in another place,
swallow their freedom whole; and they will chatter about
        their boys;
but all week and all year,
they die in gossamer cages their frail minds can never break
that once might have broken steel and stone.
I am empty of sympathy or any pity
for their shrill irritable songs.
        Turning to eagles and hawks
for paradoxes to satisfy the heart,
I think of Godwin unable to live in his own light,
of Proudhon, proofreading the 'Lives of the Saints',
of Marx in the New York Tribune—and I laugh.

A STORE-HOUSE

There is a small store-house of knowledge in which
        I sit sometimes on hard wooden cases
leaning against stacks of material kept there for use;
the door is ajar, and I can see a lawn,
some buildings, a segment of street
where people pass. But no one looks in through my door.

I sit, leaning and looking at the samplings I get
of the world; I meditate about it:
of the numbers of girls in colleges compared with men,
        and of the future of society;
of the muscles of coloured coal-heavers opening a man-hole;
of labour, power, and ignorance;
of the idiocy of avarice, of fear, and of the danger of ideals;

of the pity of people, that plod like dray-horses or senseless nuns
set on a narrow plank of purpose, with their beautiful
        wandering eyes
shielded by habit, the death and anodyne of life.

And sometimes I want to cry, and sometimes to call out,
to raise a banner before my shack, make up a congregation.
But I know that no one will look into my door—
the people pass by too busy.

        God knows, I will go out
and walk in the streets.
Perhaps I will meet other men sitting in doorways, sad as I am;
if I find them, we will sit aside somewhere
and talk this over.

A STREET IN APRIL

Look now, at this February street in April
where not a flower blossoms, or if one broke
would be like water from a blister, a yellow poke,
new bird-lime on a rail, or jet from a yolk.

Neither the fire-escapes making musical patterns
nor the filigree of stone flowery and decorating
can now accompany young April; the iron grating
jars, someone dropped a kettle in the orchestrating.

There a pale head rising from an eyeless cavern
swivels twice above the street, and swiftly dips
back into the gloom of the skull, whose only lips
are the swinging tin plate and the canvas strips.

And here are infants too, in cribs, with wondrous eyes
at windows, the curtains raised upon a gasping room,
angelic in white diapers and bibs, to whom
the possibilities in wheels and weather—bloom.

But I have seen a dove gleaming and vocal with peace
fly over them, when his sudden wings stirred
and cast the trembling shadow of a metal bird;
so April's without flower, and no song heard.

FROM A LIBRARY WINDOW

The scene is paper-thin, pastel pale and white,
the tennis courts are horizontally smooth
chalked with flat lines; the players strike
the ball with abstract sticks;
now the field tilts to an experimental plane,
the players' faces grow light red:
this is a platform, for the play of intellect.

A wind rises and sweeps the pale sand,
a Mongolian storm taking away the land.
It thrashes at the feet of the men;
yet all is simple and light-swept, the wind
sounds like the singing of humming birds,
a feeble flight we can allow or end
with a motion of the hand.

At this distance, closed in glass shelves,
leaning against each other, the realities
past and present are easy,
dispersed on a level plane, in an order of line, under the
rule of play:
but we miss the muscle wrenched from the thigh,
the eye slit by the sun racing the pin ball,
and the active brain broken by fight and defeat.

IN A STREETCAR

With brief moustache and cultured face,
Black Homburg hat, and stiff tie,
And the city edition in his hand
Scanned with an anxious or weary eye—

He edges in his allotted space,
Holding his own against the crowd,
Immaculate and silent, though
Flesh is flung round, and they are loud:

And seeking distraction from the sound,
Or from some persistent pain in mind,
He turns away with fleeting eyes
And eats his lip, as he reads a sign.

THE MOUNTAINS

In streets, among the rocks of time and weather,
with the crisp noises around, and the surrounding voices,
hearing the steel of wheels repeatedly, like bayonets,
and the sound of guns from buildings, where the windows
icily shut suddenly like visors, and men are marching;

past the trucks stooped in rows like horses
with sacks thrown tenderly over their shoulders,
the hooded and silent heroes in garages—
I walk, though the frost-fire plays in my fingers
and my eyes are crying in this freezing weather.

And amazed, I hear a few anxious voices
rise extemporizing in the hoar-frost air,
singing, on this plateau, our latest position
high in the mountains, near the dividing line
where it is coldest, and the rocks are a parapet.

Yes, soon, the hills scaled, we shall look down
into bright greenery, valleys, and rivers
thinning into wheat-fields! And the cold air like water
will flow from us, while we gaze and gaze
at the low valleys, and the meandering rivers.

O CONTEMPORARIES

In a cloud of time, this dust of locusts, in which we move
Involved with Stalins, Churchills, and chorus girls' legs,
Who is the Gulliver to shake the earth with a feather,
Unravel the tongues of the winds and make them talk?

They say any man—a locust—in every crook of his wings
Can in an empty treble, yet enough to fill a space
With the sharp, sure, useful whistle of the flywheel
Make our intelligence like the intense cricket sing;

But it fails, and frays like wire in dissonant noises,
Hurts the heart awhile, dies away, and leaves no sound;
There is no noise of knowledge left, but only the clatter
Of caricatures, a Hitler circus, jitterbugging kids.

Gather together the broken teeth of light scattered
From Rockefeller's skyscrapers, and the bones of numb neon.
Reassemble them. What records of reptiles' jaws,
What beasts are these? Take them to the museum, and ask.

Let the white-frocked boys tell you of time's serpent,
Of man in his naked skin, who is vulture and fish
And cell in a slide, like a swollen eye trailing
Out of the womb he came from like a blazing star:

But not what dimensions of space he sleeps in, what times
He sweeps as he multiplies, what gods he gives joy to;
Nor what is this storm-blind moment that we tread,
What this unsteady stone in space on which we cross.

BUILDING A SKYSCRAPER

By the street's noise muffled, the hammers
sock silently; a mittened hand
plucks concrete pieces from the ground,
throws them with a curse without a sound,
as automatic these men
building a skyscraper in the precincts of Wall street
work without being heard, without headlines, with only
a truckful of sand making rapids of applause.

Skyscrapers have their origins in the Stone Age.
Under the concrete feet of every hall,
under steel, this hammering must be done. So pausing for the bow,
these partners, prototypes of mankind consider
the hole they have made, a place to open a pail, unwrap paper
and eat ham, a cave this winter—but a bone-heap
of vapour and people next summer, a skyscraper.

And here is surprise and paradox; one of the boys
leaning on a handle sports a pipe, is no longer primitive:
the stem is silver, and a luxury of billows
expands from the bowl!

Now he folds on his belly over a steam-drill
and shakes like dead meat—but to him stones give way
and walls fall; he kicks them to hell and the crane,
makes room for a girder, for a small finger
to hold up an iron web in the air,
metallic bones hung in the velvet night,
and clothed with flesh, a hand between the moon and
        men's eyes.

The same man may rivet as well as work a drill,
may measure the dimensions, or draw a blueprint,
approve the designs and pay the bills:
but for a name and a number the same man
plans a city, and builds it, and writes it a religion.
We are identical in everything but words and clothes,
the track we took from the unequal springboard of the womb.

Tomorrow I will come and watch their progress.
I know for certain that these digging men
nudging each other with their elbows, pushing the drill left,
scoop clay from under the rump of profit and finance.
Digging here and in the next street, today or tomorrow,
something will finally happen, a bank will sag,
a building sway like a fork on a prong;
with shouting and throwing from side to side, the houses
will fall into the diggers' arms. The Stone Age will be done.

And then, a colosseum will be made of the street,
sidewalks will become benches, and windows break with cheers.
We will praise "Men Working." They will be celebrated
more than millionaires, since without rich men
nations can run as well, or better, but not without these men.
And because they now work inaudibly, cursing behind a fence,
I know that someday, over the applause and clamour
of the crowd, will fall on every ear the workman's hammer.

FLOWERS ON WINDOWS

Flowers bloom in the window pots in sprays
of softness, or pointed like pain—waves of violets,
stiff chrysanthemums, bugles, bells of red:
against the walls they are the life that answers,
they are the dwellers, and the rest is dead.

Men move mountains and build their cities;
and yet, the only answer one would like to find,
the Fact the mind would embrace as a lover
and would greedily uncover under the design—
is the city built within him that moves a man!

Though lost in the ignorant traffic, still I would rejoice.
There is some hidden wisdom in all gardens,
cities, in the leaves of flowers, the eyes of boys!
The dog is not reckless of that message, nor
are the men and women rattling through the stores.

All moves with a hidden meaning; only the fool
denies God—even as the priest-fool simplifies.
Tell me, should we see in the revolving seasons
mathematics? in the weather, circulating air?
Or the answer, then, in any book, or prayer?

What is there in man which builds a city?
And where the original city he began?
I have ravaged the womb, and the planted seed,
and moved mountains of knowledge for this gold.
Now look upon the surface—how these flowers unfold!

THE POMEGRANATE

The jewelled mine of the pomegranate, whose hexagons of honey
The mouth would soon devour but the eyes eat like a poem,
Lay hidden long in its hide, a diamond of dark cells
Nourished by tiny streams which crystallized into gems.

The seeds, nescient of the world outside, or of passionate teeth,
Prepared their passage into light and air, while tender roots
And branches dreaming in the cell-walled hearts of plants
Made silent motions such as recreate both men and fruits.

There, in a place of no light, shone that reddest blood,
And without a word of order, marshalled those grenadiers:
Gleaming without a sun—what art where no eyes were!—
Till broken by my hand, this palace of unbroken tears.

To wedding bells and horns howling down an alley,
Muffled, the married pair in closed caravan ride;
And then, the woman grown in secret, shining white,
Unclothed, mouth to mouth he holds his naked bride.

And there are days, golden days, when the world starts to life,
When streets in the sun, boys, and battlefields of cars,
The colours on a bannister, the vendors' slanting stands
Send the pulse pounding on like the bursting of meteors—

As now, the fruit glistens with a mighty grin,
Conquers the room; and, though in ruin, to its death
Laughs at the light that wounds it, wonderfully red,
So that its awful beauty stops the greedy breath.

And can this fact be made, so big, of the body, then?
And is beauty bounded all in its impatient mesh?
The movement of the stars is that, and all their light
Secretly bathed the world, that now flows out of flesh.

FLOWER BULBS

Most men give flowers in their full leaves,
But I give you flowers still in seed:
These flowers you see are each one wrapped
In the womb, still concentrated in sap.

Think, what I lay on your fearless palm!
A universe compacted to a seeming chaos,
A wary cell waiting to split its tomb
In birth, when the soon-rampant seed explodes.

Yet we generate such, and once were seeds:
Have blossomed once like flowers inside a girl;
Now sit with hanging hands and open eyes,
Nourished by, not knowing, the objective world.

And this which is closed to younger eyes
Only loving you could have opened to me.
I have walked by many a garden in a room
And passed by many a precipice being blind.

Yet love may tell one who grows a plant
How a miraculous ignorance surrounds
Each living thing—and it still be
Perfect and wise, and beautiful as a bud.

So you and I, when these plant leaves appear
Like days unfolding in the calendar,
Will watch the flowers sent out in shoots
And love grow out of his mysterious roots.

NIGHT FIRE

Heralded by the clangorous fire wagon
And bells pealing loud in the awakened night,
Boys rush out in their white shirts calling
And voices drown in red and violent sound.

Feet flash on pavements, arms signal the air,
As the fiery bell peals forth cries of "Fire!"
And mothers shriek from windows, while the churning
Long black billows on the sidewalk roll.

The crowd is sucked down alleys and past corners,
Trips over tin, swoops and picks up stones—
A mob advances to a conflagration
Where bells and water congregate in flame.

Mesmerized as if by murder, men move watching,
Under cover, half afraid, and half proud;
Coils of the fire hose loop upward and tumble,
Twitching in black tortures and in figure eights.

The smell of roofs, the odor of flesh burning,
Bite bitter at the senses aroused by death;
Mouths open, throats dry, eyes glass with dread
Fill with the fire burning through the night.

And the fire is a torch held in the night's darkness—
A frenzied joy, a fiesta, a feast of flame.
It is a blaze burning out a heavenly hole,
A hag of flame leaping and roaring hurrah.

Diamonds drip down on the floors and sputter,
Stairs fall feebly, a doorway, and now a steeple;
Burning the better for the ladders and snow water,
The flaming edifice opens out its whitened jaws—

And whining, dies in the falling of walls and boards.
The men in rubber do their duty with loud axes;
An ice-cold river finishes the fieriest coal.
It is all over now. The sour ashes are moistened,

And the last sparks fly to the tongue-thickening smoke.
In a white vapour, the ruins rise in the dawn,
Raising charred bones of love to the dying stars
That go down eastward, blue, in their black orbits.

TO A LITERARY PATRON

I once drank coffee at your sun-stained window,
Stirring around a plume of clouded cream,
While souls plumetted like stars into the river
And automobiles made swastikas on the green.

The palisades, reared by slow geological fury,
The bridge built by capital to carol for mankind,
Looked on in equanimity at your frail futility
In propping up the architectures of the mind.

Can we remember sunsets someone mentioned
Or anything whatever anybody said?
The symbols at the window sputtered louder,
As the mind plumbed the distances to things unsaid!

You urged me, later, I must try in earnest
And give my time attentively to—Art.
I knew the anger of the distant silences
Listened to the lappings of my guilty heart;

And said I would, and we drank tea or coffee;
The carvings on the table scattered ice,
And a little Jesus in a bed of amber
Grimaced at the spearpoints of electric lights.

THE PROFESSORS

Here, in a room where the great men are called,
Mountains of knowledge come, but to no Mahomet—
Bowing each other forward with burden erudition
Between white pillars to the grand dining hall,

Kit Marlowe, with Khafre's court and the beta rays,
Fight for space in the midst of verbalized encounters
Where if someone flounders, a tall and sober surgeon
Stands by to serve the beef chops, oxtails, if not praise.

Flexible in starch, like snow in marble, numb
But beautiful the Doctors, will be live as mice
Lost in an experimental maze, while down below
The lightning from the window sweeps a Harlem slum.

Rejected from the subway, not known in barber rings,
Covered in a case of glass, with words applicable
Sometimes to banks and bridges, never to lice;
Of hidden crowns, without scepter, the faineant kings;

Branching to trails that run, but cannot meet,
Their knowledge, burrowed under ground, shot from self;
Their words, voluble smoke to a blind man's eyes
That hurt, but cannot help the people in a street.

Is there not something common, all men know,
Of fathers' furrowed face, and peasants' hands—
The lineage of the blood being like—to reconcile
These poor in heart, so rich, with the poor below?

APPENDECTOMY

Beginning with an expert finger touching the abdomen,
The surgeon's certainty bows him to risk excision—
The glass doors of the hospital open to strange light;
Soon the patient is meek and waits for the razor of reason.

His animal protestations the murdering etherizer
Smothers, and leaves him senseless, at last relaxed;
Now he sleeps like a leaf on water, while a needle
Threads his insides, then closes the meaty track.

But part of his life was taken in the incision:
A retching mouth bewails the gash in his side;
Fever pouts his lips, he lies half-dead in the sand—
Two days of drought save him for a watery tide.

Morning! An early waking, and the warm washing basins;
Breakfast in bed, newspapers at his feet to scan.
The patient rises now, and feels his middle,
Totters two steps, a babe on the nurse's arm.

And so convalescence advances. Like a bird, at midday
He is hungry for the seeds of health, wise and made whole;
But he looks from the evening window at the social body
Where appendices and cysts in bloom perpetually explode.

MR. GROMYKO

Either over an empty glass at cocktail parties
or walking away from the half-circle in a gym,
slapped by the flashlights to the front covers,
he never smiled, though many smiled at him;

in armour, in the harbour of polite people,
and with a head too large and awkward hands,
he reminded one of the uncomfortable newsreels,
shy almost, like his man of steel at Teheran:

out of sorts in their society like one
checking a workman's cap among silk hats,
to whom the smiling enemy became bright crystal,
sharp irritant to the rough diplomat.

So with comical policy, crude as a noise,
he forced every issue to the point of swords,
challenged the representatives of the fair exploiters
for whom he held no compromise and no kind words;

always wrong in the considered newspapers,
fighting democracy like an unfeeling ape
he spoke a strange language like a believer
pious towards some god in a godless shape—

not unlike one who hated because he loved,
with lovers of workday hands he enjoined hate,
accusing that the rich disarm with love
and only the petty bourgeois stand and wait,

that under the legs of action the proprietors
aim the iron bolts of the established truths;
the pernicious vine sucks at the stinking tree,
the sapling is murdered by the mouldering roots.

This apologist for the red empire threatening spoke
peeling an eye at oil, sea lanes, the market dumps;

he grew pale walking between the pointed cannon,
was insolent with the peacemen righteous on their rumps;

entered a funeral home of flowers, a stench of prayer,
and prodded the corpse with his insistent cane,
roused from their incensed sleep the impenitents
to the feud still raging on the smoking plain.

He shook the curtain concealing warring empires
of the envious and angry many menacing old preserves:
the muscular soviets in plunder at the broken fences
of the gold-fobbed master's guarded fowl and hares.

Then each day, his voice guttural and anonymous
vanished like a man into a boiling mob,
became red Russia to the press; and to his people
just a fellow of the village, on a distant job.

PUERTO RICAN SIDE-STREET

Morning came at me like a flung snowball,
the light flaked out of a chalk-blue sky;
and I was walking down the dilapidated side-street
like a grasshopper in a field, just born;
all the rails and pails glistened and deceived me
with bunches of blue flowers and with silk of corn.

The yellow shades were mostly down, some up, some torn;
and I went looking into windows, into rooms,
looking for the breakfasters, and the cluttered dressers
and cracked walls; watching the black doorways and the dim
charred halls, for the baby carriages and the kids;
and as I walked, they came, like shots in a foreign film.

And then, in a blue window, lifted like a cross,
her legs straight, hair flat, and arms strung wide,
gazing out at the daylight out of coal-black
glassy eyes, I saw the twelve-year child—a saint
upon a stained-glass window—with her blue sash dress
hanging on her, thinly, and her small face thin and faint.

As I passed looking at her eyes held far away,
she almost turned; but the sun suddenly came
from behind some chimney stack, and I went ahead:
the street blazed up again. The morning hour,
that made the ashes shine and the stones burst out in flame,
had shown me in her face the sad, dark human flower.

4:

NEW MUSIC

NEW MUSIC

We make our freedom in the laws we make,
And they contain us as the laws we break
Contained a remnant of an ancient music
That a new music in its laws contains.

COMING SUDDENLY TO THE SEA

Coming suddenly to the sea in my twenty-eighth year,
to the mother of all things that breathe, of mussels and whales,
I could not see anything but sand at first
and burning bits of mother-of-pearl.
But this was the sea, terrible as a torch
which the winter sun had lit,
flaming in the blue and salt sea-air
under my twenty-eight-year infant eyes.
And then I saw the spray smashing the rocks
and the angry gulls cutting the air,
the heads of fish and the hands of crabs on stones:
the carnivorous sea, sower of life,
battering a granite rock to make it a pebble—
love and pity needless as the ferny froth on its long smooth waves.
The sea, with its border of crinkly weed,
the inverted Atlantic of our unstable planet,
froze me into a circle of marble, sending the icy air out in
        lukewarm waves.
And so I brought home, as an emblem of that day
ending my long blind years, a fistful of blood-red weed in
        my hand.

SUBURBAN PROSPECT

Blue, blue above the prim
houses where tea roses nestle and birds'
swift penmanship
runs across a lawn and a live maple:
asters, hedgerows, a yellow tree
brinded against the sky, and the houses
flawless—no cottage hanging with vine
and with time overgrown, but a Disney
design for living, a crêpe-garden at a modern door—
which a fidgety sparrow like a child at a funeral
is too much alive to know.

Here, coming at evening, you will see
Smoking Camels on the highway, and Chesterfields
ahead; maybe a Sky Chief
sign overhead—
you'll think of these as real and not instead—
General Foods will bring you wholesome breakfast
every day, a Child's
Cafeteria will serve you sunshine
from a tray: you will be wiser
and buy Kayser, you will be smart
and be thrifty
and live on less than it would cost a saint to die.

So living in a picture postcard
of hyaline trees and hedges,
the fizz of waterfalls coming to you from whisky and
lime,
in a land of Better Homes and Gardens,
a scent of cement and tile . . .
Any day, or any evening
(when the birds are making most noise),
you'll walk home to roses
hanging on your trellis, open the lock of love
with Liberty in your pocket, Life under your arm.

POEM FOR SPRING

Mother Earth's belly is broken,
        the spring begins.
Sap flows into deadened arteries,
        branches open,
the lamb bleats, the pussy willow
        puts out;
green is her blood—
        the white scab of winter is washed away.

O let this new birth be
        into a fertile year!
Let the summer fruit be a full scrotum
        between the desired branches
and not fall to the ground,
        wrinkled apples.

Let the horn of morning
        awaken sleeping feathers
                all the long summer,
and if winter comes,
        let it be a sleep
hungry, and dreamful
        of unforgotten spring.

HOT TIME

(For Herb Gold)

We played ball in the hot sun
until the sweat came down with a fine uncorking of the pores
and dripped on the scorched cement.
Then we walked up the street
and showered off;
afterwards sat naked in the room
drinking cold Coke and talking:
I read from a book about birds,
you had Joycean answers;
and we would have talked more if it hadn't been so damned hot—
but we only sat, looking at each other and laughing,
while the sun went around the world and hissed in the water.

MIDNIGHT TRAIN

Falling pell-mell in a torrent past my eyes
telegraph posts and homes
run into the infinite bag of night,
the past behind us,
in which enclosed, as from a nightmare
we have hidden within our artifice of train,
the capsule, in which all objects seem both real and whole.
But I would break through and escape from this lie
and face the night of which I am impatient, yet afraid;
I wish and wait for the sun to rise in blood
to halt the falling trees and homes,
stand all things again on their roots
and make the world turn in a great horizontal wheel,
or a road splayed up the mountain like a hand on fire.

THE TOLERANT TREES

Some conspiracy of silence among the trees
        makes the young birds secret,
or laughing at our infirmities
        in birdlike fashion, they titter in feathers;
but the uncondescending trees,
too wise to speak against us, against streamlining,
        against new fashions in uniforms and clothes,
wear always the same drab leaves,
        preserve a Sachem silence
toward our puberty rites of golf and war.

THE CHILD

The tripping of a girl just eight years old,
        a skyward leaping
up from the arches and the tiny thighs

in swings, like flying—
        springs with a laugh into living,
up from the earth, from dying.

Faustus, see
Margaret at her leaping, reaching hands;
she winds her wrists around
with blue and strikes her fists
against that tyrant who
        in a little time
will catch her at her skipping, in her sleep,
and stop all flying,
cover her with earth and down her bed
with small cold feathers from ungrieving skies.

LINE AND FORM

The great orchestrating principle of gravity
                    makes such music of mountains
as shaped by the mathematical hands
        of four winds, clouds
              yield in excellent and experimental sculpture;
mushrooms, elephants
       and women's legs, have too their form
            generated within a three-dimensional space
                      efficiently.

And so the emotions
       combine into exquisite
            counterparts of the mind and body
when the moving principle and the natural limits imposed
                  work against each other,
                        give in, and resist.

The form is then the single body
            of love that two wrestlers make.
But has each one his own?
                        or is one?
What essential form has
                  a wind or the sky
that cutting into each other
                       they mimic living arms?

Eternal forms.
The single power, working alone
       rounds out a parabola
               that flies into the infinite;
but the deflected particle
            out of that line, will fetch a frisk
                      of sixes and eights
                           before it vanishes:

an ocean arrested
by sudden solid
ripples out in the sand.

So this world of forms, having no scope for eternity,
is created
in the limitation of what would be complete and perfect,
achieving virtue only
by the justness of its compromises.

LOVERS

The daughters of the moon and sun
Have shoulders like green apples
And mouths of flame:
The sons of thunder lie with them

In the magnetic mountains.
Rivers of mercury trickle down the rocks
Where the maidens lie on the mosses
With the boys born out of lightning.

RELATIVITY

The sparrows bathe in the dust
in the soft sun,
male birds quivering in warmth and
pecking at the fluffy
mothers;

Cornus (dogwood) quivers on the stems,
known
by its winter characters;

and *Pyrus* (mountain ash) in March
by the buds
and spines, the tender red and green
buds (if you look close) and the small
spines.

A quiver in Space-Time, they say
is the definition of man;
a quivering
Continuum, the definition of nature.

SPACES

The seven stars
of the Great Wain
hang in the sky
a million light years
one from another
and from me, but I
gather the seven together
who could never know
me or one another
but for my human eye.

ORIGINAL

'Look!' said a child, at 'blue water',
pointing at a sky-patch over the town.
Water is sky, and sky water. Pure
perception cannot be wrong. I say
'sky-blue', and that original, an old
perception, begins to glide—sky and water,
the earliest emblems of a sensible world.
Hauled into one, resolved into many,
the fragment world is held together
like fish that flash, in identification's net.

METAMORPHOSES

Yesterday's snow,
            ten white handkerchiefs
                        on the grass.
At sunset
            geese will rise
                        across the moon;

or whirled out of a locomotive,
            clouds explode
                        over tons of iron.

MOUTHS

Pendulous mouth, you flap in a wind
            on a space-washed skull,
make a wilderness of sound

            brlaa
              brlaa frloo

flapping mouths
          on wind-swept heads—
until two cross to close the gap
between all art and artery, heart and the empty world
            lubb lubbu luvbl
              aluvu

close each other with a skill or will
under that spell
to loose themselves into each other,
              then turn to lose themselves
in that greater mouth
            nothing can still or fill.

TAKING SHAPE

Taking shape
          (wings)
              of pigeons

make a temporary, a true
          forever continued
              perfection!

So everywhere
whatever moves, whatever settles
rises on feet, or wings
takes its shape;
ungrace is its undoing,
a fear to fall,
defection;

so consonants close
(wings!) in a whorl
of vowels—

the same
and different
birds in other trees.

THE MOMENT

The poet who begins to write no poem,
he is the one I want to be.
Having no need to give
of himself, and not convinced others need
or would, in any case, take
it, he is free.
A poet beginning just to be.
How smooth, and clean,
this thought appears to me!
The table has been cleared, a piece
of paper on it . . . I sit and laugh
at the beauty of my white
freedom for the act—
reluctant to end,
in decision, this perfect thing.
You who are curious,
will have to wait and see!

THE JUNGLE

Time has its ends and its beginnings—
    leaf-end and stem, skin and liver—
through which the rhythm passes,
    a drum-beat in a jungle silence,
somewhere in the trees the shriek
    of a wild bird shattered by claws,
somewhere the big cats mating, crying
    in pain, possibly in delight,
and the silence is endless, listening to the drums
    day after day with a new beginning,
day after day anguish, possibly pleasure,
    but beyond that the perfect white of the sky
waiting above the world for the movement to cease,
    to be absorbed in the folds of its sea,
to be drowned in space where all that was
    is sound in a deaf ear, fear in a forgotten dream.

THE GREAT AS IF

If I die, love,
(as I must)
it is as if I had not been;

and for me, then,
this world
will be as if it had not been.

But who is less unreal?
You too will die,
we must all die, as if we had not been.

What, then, was this life?
Where was this world—
when all will be as if it had not been?

QUARREL

Bitch
Beast Buffoon Egoist
Catface
You.

Emerald eyes
your forehead is white as a September morning
but I have grown tired of loving,

even your beauty
can no longer move me,

like an autumn leaf
you wither in my eyes to ashen grace.

Why should we quarrel then?
Let us kiss
and put wisdom into each other's mouth.

ON SUDDEN DEATH

I have seen old men and some young men go
stumbling into a field of wind, in heaving grass,
mild people, whose loss was like all human loss;
but he was a proud man for death to lay so low.

He wouldn't have wanted to know how it happened;
would have looked angry, stubborn as he was,
at the cheap trick death played him; also because
his dead body was helpless to answer or resent it.

For he was proud, like all who lord the beast
with more-than-human dignity, simple as fact;
proud neither in thought nor in talk, but in act—
till death laid this insult on his swollen chest.

He would not bend, to life's indignity and pain:
so mindless death, ungenerous, unexpected came.

THE DEAD

After we knew that we were dead we sat down and cried
  a little, only we found that our eyes were now empty
  and we were without any feeling of sadness.
'We had it coming, it was bound to happen,' said one.
'I am thinking of the future,' said a lady beside him.
'There is no future,' an old man affirmed.
'I'm glad,' said one, looking back toward the earth. 'I'm
  free of it, I'm no longer one of them. I am glad.'
'So am I' someone echoed.
'So am I.'
'So am I . . . So am I,' the echo traveled along the plain and
  beyond. I did not know whether it was an echo, or
  whether others were there repeating the sound.
'So am I, so am I' . . . it went on, the whole valley and plain
  resounded.
I turned my eyes around to see, but there was only a grey
  transparency without end, and empty, that was like
  a wall before me. I could see as far as I wanted but
  I wanted to see nothing, and there was nothing.
One of the dead beside me stirred, and as if a memory had
  awakened him he said, 'They are always on edge down
  there. We were always on edge.'
'And there was also the fear of death,' said a man of
  middle age.

'Someone there dies every day, every hour.
Think of the bird in the teeth of the hunter, beating its wings, crying out—
That was the way we were.' He fell into a deep silence. We all sat for a long time in silence.
Below us stretched the endless plain, and in the foreground, still near, the earth hung, like a sad town in a grey mist.
'There they sit, the beautiful women and the young men in their prime; time passes over them, and they shrivel in ugliness, looking at one another in amazement. O, I am glad to be out of it. Glad to be rid of it.'
'But the worst is that even the innocent suffer,' said a lady.
'They are all innocent,' the old man muttered.
Then, raising his head, one poor skinflint beside me made a face like a devil who had done a good deed, and said, 'All this is important. I never worried about important things. The worst of it was, as I see it now' . . . (he looked out across the plain into the grey distance without obstacle) 'was to be caught in a net that did not even exist.'
'When you are caught in a net,' said the man of middle age, 'whether it exists or doesn't exist, it is still a net, and you are caught in it.'
'I don't even want to think of it,' said the wizened man, as if losing interest;
'I remember,' and here he bit his lip out of ancient habit, 'that even love was painful.'
And just as he said this, a dark cloud passed over us, and the earth was blotted out.
It brightened. But the figures beside me, and the earth that had formed a dark figure, receded, in no determinate direction, until I could see no longer. And then we were bathed in a morning light of sudden gladness. And there was nothing.

5:
SELECTIONS FROM EUROPE

SEA AND LAND

1

Cleaving out through the clean St. Lawrence,
cellophane sweeps crisp with contemporaneity,
the shores receding . . .
                    going out to sea. . .

                              Bridge
parties in the lounge,
        and tourist chatter:

Time's newest, flimsiest, cheapest crinkles
      unwrapping Vacation Tours—
"Let's finish this hand"
            "I've had enough"

Travelling tourist class, to Europe
        out of American, Canadian cities.
What are we going to find?
      What are we going to see?

2

This is not yet the sea, it is the river.
For a long time we have been
only on the river, the rocking-horse waves
of a minor reality, Newton's invention:
roof slates on a mechanical surface,
dollar bills of green, small froth of holiday beer
            and ice-cream soda.

The river between green banks
holds in the mocked tide
beyond Quebec, beyond Megantic, Restigouche.

Dotted with Donald Duck villages
the shore mounts like a flapjack
on either side. Bridged here and there by cantilevers,
scooped by the dredger, man.

Nowhere is it so noisy, nowhere so unnatural & noisome
as (singing some yoo-ooo love song)
here on this river; yet it is the realest thing,
your present, a gift of time,
the tamed moment of eternity
                                        for you,
flowing on and out into the sea, where we go.

3

Even on a river you will find great puddles of froth
                        trying to beat up a sea.
Even in June an occasional ice-floe (was it?)
                            or a sea-gull's wing.

A river tears down its banks and graves its deepest ruts
as deep as it can, bores away, chasm to peneplane
before it gives way and gives in.
                                A river is a member of the sea;
of sky-sperm, sky fathered, flowing down free
                                        to its blood-purple parent.

4

The biggest waves in this water
are those we make ourselves.

But why fish
in someone else's backwash?

There was a time when I was satisfied
with fishing in the clean St. Lawrence,
the Little Jesus River
(no sooner Souster heard it
but he put it in a poem),
whiskered bullheads, sweet slim perches,
soup fish in summer.
"Ca mord-t-il?" we used to shout
to the fishermen under the bridge.

A plodding sport, for the trivial imagination,
of waiting, waiting—
then it comes, a small civilized
fish
that dies practically in your hand.

Can you live—or die—for such pleasure?
If you have grown to manhood
and strong reaching desire?
Yet there are people
who want no other art, or life
(though there's no profit in it)
—weekends little better than a long sleep,
or walking in sleep.
Like Bob, who made it a point of pride
to catch a five-pound pike in any water!

How to lure out the last sleeping whopper
out of a pond—yes, there's "art" in that.
But where we go, there are no shores.

5

Quebec lives by the river, by the slim St. Lawrence.
But for the river, Champlain
would not have found it,
Cartier would not have gone so far,
nor La Salle settled. The ocean liner

comes here and takes us out,
takes wheat, silver, paper;
and the fish come here,
fresh fish, that taste best salted, the sea fish,
the sea salmon, that dies in the mountains.

The river made these cities. Last night
the Chateau and its brood of houses
stood for a moment in soft pastel colours
            on the sky as we passed;
then the lights beyond it a *via lactea*,
stretching for miles beyond, and Lévis,
both in the mouth of the St. Lawrence,
shone—the river buttons; the rest, night
        cloaking a cold continent.

Three Rivers is named for it, and raids on the land
as well as on the ocean, stripping forests.
                                        Montreal
raids on the world for population,
Hungarians, Poles, Mongolians, Greeks and Jews,
as well as the two conventional races
who stiffen against each other in their pride.
            Too much to lose!

The river brings them its mixed blessings,
other people's broken wrongs; brought its
accumulation of dead habits,
the racial tics of other nations.
Prisoners, castaways, the poor, the malcontents
                    came to the colonies.
Raw matter for a raw country,
too often wasted and withered there, unused, left to dry.

9

Land is delightful, whatever islands,
St. Pierre & Miquelon,
whatever mountains

we pass, are delightful and habitable places
we look at wondering
how it would be there
to fish there, hunt, set up houses,
whether cities will spring up someday
in the Shickshocks,
in tracts of Newfoundland,
already, see, there are people
there, there
St. Pierre & Miquelon, fishing islands
(French still, 1660/1814, taken, ceded)
the last we shall see,
and then the sea. . . .

10

But I had not known the sea would be this splendid
magnificent lady:
"destroyer of ships, of cities"
in luxurious ermine and leopard coat
sighing in the ship's wake;

destroyer of civilizations, of pantheons,
to whom Greece and Rome are only a row of white breakers
spilled with a hush, in air,
then marbled patterns on a smoother wave. . .

And I would not be surprised if the sea made Time
in which to build and to destroy
as it builds these waves and indolently breaks them,
or if the whole fiction
of living were only a coil in her curvature
of immense imagination.

Maker and breaker of nations, sea of resources,
you have enough here for a million rivers,
for a billion cities,
enough for new Judea, for new Alexandria,
and Paris once again, and America's morning.

11

New men and new women!
—The sea is so easily bored!
And treacherous . . . in love . . .
like any woman.
Beware, O nations, of her coiled and serpentine body.

12

Here the dead are very familiar,
Davy Jones and all his fellows,
those who walked the plank and died in storms
or plummeted down in silent coffins.
The sea has swallowed so many
(and what is land if not a crust of its selvage,
earth swallowing its dead, doing the sea's business . . .)
The dead become very familiar,
Shelley, Edward King,
commemorated,
those athletes on the Titanic,
all the Olympians, of Salamis, Trafalgàr—
familiar. And to the victor
a crown of white foam and these cheers
over and over again.

14

Columbus with all kinds of cockeyed notions
just had to keep on going and he was sure to find it,
the alchemists with all kinds of cockeyed notions. . .
Explore the sea for any reason,
and you are bound to come upon treasure.
Keep active, persist in folly,
just keep on going,

keep mixing, even with your hands.
The sea has everything, it's the globed universal belly
bulging with wombs.

17

'Just a lot of water,' someone says.
But when the seas begin to dry
the earth itself will become parched
and bare as the moon.

This water contains its living animals
and all the living animals the world contains
come from this water . . .

All that is good in us is still whatever of the sea
we contain.

19

The commotion of these waves, however strong, cannot disturb
the compass-line of the horizon
nor the plumb-line of gravity, because this cross coordinates
the tragic pulls of necessity
that chart the ideal endings, for waves, and storms
and sunset winds:
the dead scattered on the stage in the fifth act
—Cordelia in Lear's arms, Ophelia, Juliet, all silent—
show nature restored to order and just measure.
The horizon is perfect,
and nothing can be stricter
than gravity; in relation to these
the stage is rocked and tossed,
kings fall with their crowns, poets sink with their laurels.

21

From eleven every morning the program reads "Concert",
but it turned out to be Be-Bop
        exclusively and German *Sehnsucht*
of Nelson Eddy vintage.
                "How about Mozart?
                                Or The Messiah?"
piped an American collegian.
                                "Let's relax!"
The intellectual calibre (high on this voyage)
is about that of the Sat. Eve. Post
but as for entertainment the same
does for all "cattle" (the trade name for passengers).
            What does the sea care
regarding the noise we make?
The sea does not care,
but it makes its meaning plain:
crossing the ocean swell to jazz rhythms
we are certainly a Ship of Fools!

The sea is the only measure of music.

22

Having boarded the ship as an innocent
I had not realized that an ocean crossing
is one of our fucking institutions,
the top deck at night is a Coney Island,
cocktails whirling in crazy currents
every night in the dancehall, a shipboard romance
is part of everybody's business,
who's making who tonight, that's the question,
we are all caught in the damned human maelstrom,
forgetting the ocean, the thing doesn't matter
except as a place to feel ourselves adrift in
in every sense, cut off from the outer,

the worlds on either side, free to go nuts with
this modern idea of pleasure
creating a temporary eight-day culture
without a chance of survival
beyond the immediate present,
a freak wave in the shilly-shallying water,
not to be repeated, certainly soon forgotten.

But I have never passed up an opportunity,
and who cares how a society gratifies
the rollicking "free rhythms" of the umbilicus
so long as it does so, let's be conventional,
the waves around here have certainly started something,
with two hundred interesting bodies (and one or two minds)
to pick from, one ought to be satisfied: Darling,
just lay your head against my shoulder and the sea
will do the rest, sex at least can be satisfactory and simple.

23

Much of the time now we forget that we're moving on water.
There's no more need to be always aware of the sea
                                        than there is to be aware of the land.
It's there. It won't go away.
That's just the trouble with trying to pretend
it's not, in order to cure your small private headache.
Our stomachs are now settled.
We don't mind stumbling against each other
                                    in the corridors.
So even Fools are eventually
                                                assimilated;
there is no object so lopsided
                    but it has an exact centre of gravity.
No one is rejected
from nature. That's why
                    we suffer so for our mistakes.

G

25

Strange, that in the midst of all this deep-
sea novelty and nonsense
I think of someone far away
at the end of the world
where we started,
crossing Dominion Square from St. Antoine
or eating lunch on St. Catherine
and looking so sad
you'd think the whole world was dying
and this was his sister,
then she unties the tight little bow-knot
of her mouth
and sparks out like a small red firecracker
—till you'd think it was
the last Victoria Day—
and you know from that small bang
how wonderfully youth has advanced ahead of us
with new explosives
and the world-wrecking business.

26

It's a small world, a very small world
we move in,
but it takes us by the heart,
takes us in
before we know it, and we hate to part with it.

The gesture was really significant,
on new land, we thought it important
and we took pictures, of each putting his first foot on it.

Meeting and parting, the champagne
of life goes to these occasions.

We have left our world, we have left America,
and we are here.

ENGLAND

27

A city is a kind of ship,
most of it an old tramp
most of it salt-eaten
sea-stained, encrusted
with lives beyond recall;
some of it new
decked with modern apartments
flying flags and bunting
for life's excursion pleasures;
much of it freight and trade.

A city is a kind of ship,
it touches the ports of time—
Past and Present—the wharves of space
—Here and Now—it comes and goes
making its long voyage
and then sinks in the sand:
Troy, Ecbatan, buried cities.

28

Southampton

Ruins are beautiful,
          the city was half demolished
                                        by bombs
At first we did not understand
why all the signs of demolition, stumps
          of houses, overgrown with grass

Ugly city, we said,
if you had the choice of living
          here or living all your life on shipboard
it would be hard to choose which
                    would be less uncomfortable—
not that both don't have their points.
The horticultural side of England,
                              tiny gardens
before the dingiest of houses,
                    roses and exotic silly trees,
quaint, at once, let's hope for all
And that class deference
               which puts you in your place, up or down,
                              once for all
But for the most part, the sordid and depressing habits
               of the poor, accustomed to be poor.

A city of wharves sloppy with the sea,
                                   Southampton
City of old decrepitude and new vulgarity
Ugly city, I said
until I saw the ruined churches, weeds growing
                    on the broken walls
and understood the demolitions.

Ruins are beautiful
We will see some more glorious, more renowned
                              than these
But the ugly, like the strong, who have suffered
                         are beautiful,
And bombs have done this much for contemporaneity.
I think of the black eggs falling
                         out of the sky
and their furious spawn
                    (we bought a leather hand-grip
from a dealer bombed out of the corner block
                                   he once had)
And it is pleasant to see how right and decent
                    after all, this town is—
more real, and in the present, because death has touched it.

29

I guess nature, uncultivated, precedes us
not without form,
                    but the Sussex downs
have had two thousand years of it—
English culture. Even the fields could not remain
                                        uncivilized
after that. Nature
is lovely here, a garden, in England.
The shape one gives the land
                                    is conventional:
a sentimental culture
        like the English whose secret, common sense,
leaves no room for reality
                                  of imagination
makes even nature cosy, the oaks parks,
a landscape weeping like a watery Turner.

31

The ignorant present has scribbled over the past
                                                at Winchester;
an American goon
painted on the door
        saying "yak yak" to all this
rectangular, proud English Gothic.

At first there was nothing, the beginning
was hardest, then what they made
      was made out of what they had begun.
No matter. The present is shaped out of the first
          shaped stones,
                    from Stonehenge to this.

It is all flowers within
          and fluted stems,
"Music," you said, and "One cannot believe

it is of stone," such intricate
articulations
of white bone, and terrible black
medieval magic.

But there is nothing,
nothing in the 19th century additions:
the recent cemetery sculpture
beside the older, somber, Norman Gothic
that did not try to be beautiful.
Only true.
To what? Consider for instance
the harrowing tomb of Richard Fox
showing his body
lacerated by suffering and death,
there to tell you
—do not be too gay, even if God
doesn't particularly matter,
the bones remain, they are the cathedral.

But several tourists
have scrawled their names
on the breast of Richard Fox
just where the skeleton comes through the skin.
Let these additions remain
in Winchester
Perhaps time will prove
such fools, like sculptured animals
belong here after all.
They would have had no stone
to write so plainly on, if death had not offered them
its bony breast.

33

Courtesy is pleasing, saves us from barbarism.
In London, a frozen whirlpool of purple water,
courtesy is the memory of whispered spray
and gentleness that once smoothed the waters.

One sees the kings in wax, the Lords' seats
in Westminster, the fashionable cathedral
built by Wren, and the squares where Addison's
feet may have stepped; Gainsborough at the Tate;

sentiment and vacuity in English art, blame it
on the eighteenth century, blame it on respectability.
What is left of it, in crowded Trafalgar Square
& by bombed banks in Fleet Street, is a kind of softness

in a dying culture, saving the last good thing
before the onslaughts of unconformity come
and free unreason. But kindness is very welcome.
And what more pleasant than well-bred English people?

35

The black excrement of the factories,
Birmingham, Manchester
                    for miles and miles
smears over the country,
so dismal we must hide our eyes
from rows of silent buildings, old rust, new grime.
If ever they leave ruins
          black crickets only will sing their praise.
What is England? The beautiful gardens
               of Sussex, the Lakes,
are not her empire, her power;
it is this monstrous dream
we have tried to traverse quickly, at night,
              which still haunts our morning
with brick, with smokestacks,
          the nightmare reality we cannot shake,
which is her victory, the dark angel
               of our world.

36

Lancaster

Here you can sit and understand
how one building can civilize a city,
                    and the stalls of the Priory
hoary but always new
          (like Shakespeare's every word,
          good as when it was written)
make them rugged but kind.
They have built even their stables and garages
of that stone, and the streets are all architecture.
Old England is in this corner.
And I prefer it to Oxford.
          It is more common, still unpossessed
by those who would use beauty
                    for an advantage.
There is such a thing as being over-civilized.
          But one building
is enough, where people are receptive and somewhat rude.

37

Wordsworth certainly picked it, the best part of England
          for the sort of thing he wanted.
I had not thought it would be this
                    sensational.
The rest of England is quiet countryside, flat to the east,
                    rolling hills southward;
Cornwall and Wales have mountains, but here
          the surprises make one laugh—
a parody of romantic scenery, now highly cultivated
          and trimmed like the French poodle
with rock fences, hedges. Holiday travel
          has put a premium on the town houses,

motor coaches stream in and out of the steep hills, crowded
with nature lovers.
Here you see what a poet can do to real estate:
though that was clear to be seen at Stratford.
Wordsworth has outdone Shakespeare, by making his poems
as sizeable and safe as these mountains.
That's why the English love him. Though I doubt
whether many today who holiday here
think much in passing of his name.

40

There is something disturbing in being again on water,
I ask the white sea
if there is life anywhere
as foaming, as glowing green, as this;
if land can possibly be, or have,
ever, all that the sea contains.
Monuments fool us, delude us into believing
that once there was energy
married with equity, to raise such buildings.
But there also was pride and oppressive power,
there also (a dungeon, stocks and irons) they built for killing.
The commonplace and the brutish, serf and master
and proud priest; rotting straw on thatched roofs,
slit homestead walls of an ancient farm—
this dirt of the past may as well be cleaned out.
Why should we ride into eight hundred years ago
to see others as foul as ourselves?
If now only the proud cathedrals remain,
it is because art
outlives inhumanity.

History is really the study of failures,
the best buildings
lack some points of proportion, dimension.
Only the sea makes her circle perfect.

FRANCE

41

Across the level fields of France
extensive as empire or continent
                    the wind over the wheat
runs in delicate timid waves, moonlit in daytime.

They cultivate every acre
                with geometrical exactitude
as they built their cathedrals with grace.
            We found this true.

The beautiful mind of the cultivated Frenchman
                    must be like these fields, these waves,
an undulation measured like the dance
                            of Cleopatra's body.

42

I suppose that what you see
depends on who you are.
                    A busload of tourists
stopped by the cathedral of Amiens without looking
        at it at all, went in for coffee or to piss,
not one stood in the blazing sunlight looking upward.
                        When they rode away
we were left in the dust they raised, our eyes itching
                    from that savage crystal,
with the great round window in the dark waiting.

47

In the Place de la Concorde, where the guillotine stood
                    and did so much good
and did so much harm, we walked arm in arm

and got lost in the Louvre
that royal museum
with all those great bargains in art-books and cards.
King Louis in marble stood by then and smiled
at how we presumed
to look unimpressed by the size of his rooms
(so different the Renaud from his coach-and-six,
different the traffic from tumbrils and sticks),
but in the Place
de la Concorde six days later
the familiar tables were turned
once more, & a broken bottle hissed
as the bullets shot by the police
hit or missed.
All to demonstrate . . . what? . . . (King Louis smiles)
—that there is still no peace, but a sword,
in the Place de la Concorde.

48

Paris, more stinking royal then any city:
city of republicans, of the Conciergerie, Bastille!
(Some 10,000 visit Versailles on a Sunday?
Nothing but sentiment. O the great age
of the Roi Soleil!)
The city is filled with palaces and baroque horrors
and such filthy flamboyant statues
as deface the corners of the best cathedrals,
even Chartres—
eighteenth century additions, twentieth century
legs et dons.
And buried under Paris, under the Palais de Justice,
under St. Germain & the Louvre,
you will find the stained glass
of the Sainte Chapelle,
and a small Greek church of very early date,
and St. Séverin, perfect and harmonious, and quiet,
and the staring face of Notre Dame.

50

The Greeks were fine, but French classicism
using the Greek for its own purpose,
smooth hypocrisy, conceit, & the display
of that corruption, *le bon goût*,
—the worst taste in manners or in art
the world has ever seen—
spoiled two centuries of European art,
opened the arts to worse corruption still—
the monstrous sugar teeth
of 'money' and 'amusement': here you see
in Chartres
art is no entertainment, it does not amuse;
money paid for it, but it paid for
something that the sculptor really preferred;
pride was satisfied, but it was pride
in objects, the full scale
of human performance—they worked for this, gladly.
The wedge of ignorance entered Europe
with a blind idolatry
of Greece and Rome; you can see it
as a straight line from the 15th century down,
"art for art," copying the Greek forms,
shape without sense, imitating
imitations, dramatic motion, sensuality
for the boudoir, decorativeness
to make room for gold, for size.
After this, there was no honesty
whether in art or trade, to fight off the incizor
of the pure profiteer, the hog
with his snout in the mire, his belly in shit.
The Gothic tower had fallen,
the last craftsman
dropped his hammer; it has come
to all of us, poets, advertisers,
dance hall singers and all,
we make our pilgrimage to Chartres, without praying beads;
look at the Virgin helpless, and up to the great dome
where the light seems to rise and fall.

51

The French, as to intellect, are nothing
very exceptional, i.e., the common
man, la classe ouvrière, very pleasant, illiterate
as everywhere, the difference
is in their very marked character, habits
going back for centuries no doubt, such as
inaudible syllables, shrugs and gestures,
the closing of shops at uncustomary hours—
"to hell with business"—the head-dress at Chartres,
however, was really affected, for purposes of selling
hand-made mittens (you bought a pair),
and of course the habit
of wines and bidets, since nature,
said Pascal, is the first habit; but as to intellect
it comes to very little; and where, one might ask
does even that come from? An exceptional
individual, as in America? A concealed
aristocracy, not in these towns and villages?
The only part of intellect worth attending
is the local and popular, what you see
in the market, the streets—Utrillo
had it all handed to him, Cocteau
no doubt in the cafés learned it,
brilliant in consequence, a way of talking.
So these people are really artists, like the chambermaid
who talked a musical score, in Paris,
like the boy who danced on a bicycle.
"A city of clowns"; but a clown
is a poet in action, says Henry Miller.
Only in the country, is it depressing
to see the clowns-out-of-work, the sad
panorama of a deserted circus.
France, like any modern nation,
keeps all its valuables in one city.

52

After the thirteenth century it all deteriorates.
Three centuries
of show-off excesses
and smooth shellacking, introduce the baroque.
They discovered the Gothic
prayerful arches
at first flat and ascetic
as at Chartres, the facade
and the plain tower;
then to glorify the Virgin, or Christ
or the city (it may be) that made it,
flamboyant, glittering with jewels,
fluting and fanning upward,
splitting up the light with colours.
This was Gothic: expelling evil spirits
out of the gables,
e.g., a cat on the corner, turning his head toward you,
or animals eating each other.
By the seventeenth century, the smoothies
had learned how to cut an arch
or a cornice with the brainless exactitude
of precision instruments,
and made them all alike: one sees it
in the chapel at Amboise
where Leonardo's body lies, though part of the doorway,
the carving, is true, in the old style,
the rest is repetition, pattern without significance,
animals no longer endearing
or brutal,
simpering virgins in contemporary dress—
French, as Europe has known it
for these 300 years of French pseudo-culture.
Look at the French
Renaissance and the eighteenth century,
look at "toilet tile gothic"
and nineteenth century *gloire*, *empire*—
"classicism."
But they are not to blame;

we have come into disgusting centuries
where everything grows worse perpetually,
the sewage floating on the tide
where the white wave was broken.
And only now
only now we begin to see, begin with despising
all that bad taste
and monarchic idiocy, that corruption
in man and society through 500 years;
only now, looking for one or two
objects or men, in all Europe,
the few who work from the centre
wrestling with the evil before them
in what they say, making the words
ring true to nature—
we seem to turn on the foetid tide
of history,
making for clean water.

Not Catholic, but universal,
this vision,
no existentialist betrayal
of Pericles or Copernicus:
to carve the line
positive and true
in the smallest detail, and in the large
harmonious with the body;
to follow the rise and fall of the greater tide.

53

Under the rocks at Biarritz
where the sea rushes in, in terraces
of white breakers
toward the tourists scattered on the crisp spattered sand—
the two protagonists of this epos,
the latter creating
hotel fronts
& zebra umbrellas

as usual;
the sea carving the architraves of the ragged rocks.

Beauty is a form of energy.

When that is depleted, pleasure
          or comfort, is all that the organism desires.
The apparent energy of the factories
          and industrial sites, so ugly,
        which we have seen in France and in England
                (the length and breadth of them)
is really exhaustion, not power, so far as the worker
      is concerned, in his dismal dwellings;
despair because there is no beauty.
And the masters of that system, whom we can now see, if we
    want to,
            will be brutal beings, desperate
in their ignorant search for enjoyment and power;
they cannot be dedicated
or happy in the expression
          of their virility,
nor feel in their veins the sea as they work.
Hence the rich are great drinkers
of hard liquor, and come to these resorts
wearing short trousers,
having shaved their legs cleanly,
their arms like coffee.
They sit confidently
in deck chairs, or under tents
listening to the tame ocean,
while all Europe is a heap of ruins
covered over with new buildings; new voices
      fill the air where the hammer
chipped the rock once, the bell tolled
serenely. We take the spray on our faces
        like tiny tears
from that great duct which is green and golden.
Can you hear?
The sea is angry, because they have deceived her
            and lied to her.

THE WARM SOUTH

55

Yes, you should come south, to the warm south,
from which all Europe is visible:
San Juan de Luz, Pamplona
(the tops of Spain),
mountains, from which all Europe is plain;
the German middle
in her intestines,
and there, the cerebral madness
of the new life in Russia, where men are implored
to love the proletariat,
my darling.
In France the deserted villages,
and in England no villages at all.
Look closely
and you will see
the morning smoke of the big cities,
so unpleasant to enter,
so good to leave behind
(they have everything
that modern man desires, especially
shopping centres, depots, hoards of news);
you will see them empty of vision,
and the despair of *tous les jeunes*,
some turning to God, some to post-Kantian ethics,
LIBÉREZ chalked on the walls—
but not for these inhabitants
whose despair itself may be hopeful, if they will come and see
someday, how dirty their life was
(the young, the hostellers)
and watch the children play in the sand
and wade here in the water.

What they will do then, nobody knows;

it may be something simple
like building Chartres,
or laying down a stone.

O yes, you should come south
to see the sun rise over Pamplona
for the fiesta,
and see the sky brighten
and hear the cock crow in the Pyrenees.

59

Where the sea smashes
on the rocks at Bordighera:
simply for pleasure,
like the surf at Sete,
alone, for miles and miles
of wind and sea-washed
sand

a strip of land, where there is water on both sides
and a good road running by the sea—
lonely, we stopped and stripped
for the sweet salt surf, the sea
that took us in as though we were nothing
(making that poem)

or on the glittering Riviera
(hard pebbles, but good water)
where there are 30 miles also devoted entirely to pleasure,
we rested at any rate, one afternoon
and slept there
(the Casino stupid and vulgar,
one could see the money
raked in by the croupier,
and very little coming back)
or at *baccarat*, each betting against the other,
the House always collecting its dividends.

No art out of this, says Ezra,
there is no art where there is theft on the community
and each bets against the other.
No art in St. Raphaël,
                    Nice or Cannes,

a hundred years later, 200 years later
these villas will lie in ruin
still an eyesore
        & the money and the bankers
                                                    no more
(says, or might say, Ezra);

but we enjoyed it
lying on the beach there and sleeping
after Spain, the fiesta,
after the ruins of Villafranca,
                            the caves of les Baux,
                                    vineyards, the grape country
of Spain and France, equally good
                    and the small towns of Provença.

Lay by the sea sleeping
with the Casino overhead,
            and the sea lapping quietly at our feet.

60

You will know by their arts,
                            the fruits of a civilization.
Honest minds, like the Communist
we met at the plage with his family,
do a lot of good to make one confident
                                        at least in the ferment
within the present; but what people have left
                        or what they are now building
speaks from the heart and from the centre
                                                of any community,

whether it is railroads or warehouses
(the incomplete sentence) or villas
like a rotten egg-plant
that cannot last because they are not true
to nature, to man, what he must
and what he would like to attain.

61

A woman prefers the sea;
but I have never enjoyed swimming
as on the left side of the fiume Magra
close to the bridge
where the clear mountain water
runs no higher than your neck
and on a hot day the stream ripples cool and smooth
in the sun, by the cropped grass-bank
where we sat and talked,
& I wrote some lines, and Italy was there.

62

In the middle of the night they burst out singing,
like drunken men everywhere, I thought,
and your nerves were overwrought;
but they had a guitar, & the player was no slouch,
and they loved their songs, though the wine
had unstrung their voices;
it was this also that I had expected
(kept us awake for an hour),
like the people of Pamplona dancing,
the art that is better than poetry
or even the oldest ruins—
the art we dream of in the others.

63

A girl with a load of hay on her head,
another leading a donkey . . .
But slowly one comes to realize
that the Europe we have come to see,
of old art, stored antiquity
and the beautiful customary life
of towns and villages,
hardly exists at all;
everywhere, has given place to the new Europe,
as in Spain
the decrepit pueblo beside the modern city:
a sort of international Americanism
which is not at all American perhaps
but the face of the new life everywhere
(first grasped there
where nothing stood in the way,
except stiff colonialism
and the unhereditary aristocracy
of the Adams's and Lowells):
of factories, "the new-rich Milanese,"
and commercial storefronts.
As in Genoa, never good for art,
that defeated Pisa,
says Baedeker,
(judge the decay of the tourist intellect,
the old guides against the new blue books—
where do the French girls strip
for *exhibition*, where are the night clubs:
"What to See What to Do in Paris");
Genoa is greasy and full of business
of the kind already familiar,
except that the old streets
are still as narrow
as when they built San Lorenzo,
and they do sell
Pindemonte's Omero
at half a dollar.
Though we have come here to see old Europe,

it is the new which really concerns us,
here as in America.
The past speaks in the remaining monuments
and a few pages
of the dead poets,
judging the Esso empire
and the new Milanese
without mercy.
What should we say, we few,
who know what we know,
but for these records?
Where would we get words
for our recriminations?

64

Our eyes are filled with arches, with marble colonnades,
campaniles and towers;
when I close my lids I see them
vibrating in the after-image
their fixity has made, since the flesh tries helplessly
to preserve such stillness:
a toy model of Pisa
stirs in the million-watt sun
on the Piazza, the Florentines
walk about in purple tunics
as whimsical as their tall crenelated towers;
I see Siena shake in the sun, a white façade
blazing with immense beginnings
So this Renaissance was a third thing,
different from the Greek, or the Gothic,
imitating, only to be more itself—
a multi-pinnacled and curious city.
It must be that the kinds of beauty are infinite;
though we have tried only a few.
I think of the courtiers and "portraits of young men"
so plentiful in the galleries,
gentlemen, as there are none now, and those who could command,
—the condottieri and cavalieri, in arms

                                    or simply holding a city in the hand—
they no longer exist, Italy
might be a new race, a new people,
as they in their turn were different
                              from the Romans they so admired.
                                                                  The bawling Italian
in rags, with democratic manners, is certainly a strange curator
of such records: the fees in the museums
are higher than in France, and the guides
one hears everywhere, vulgar in their methods.
Communism is on the walls VOTA COMUNISTA,
                                    P.C.I., the names of politicians:
though unlike the loud inscriptions
of France, they seem to be the emotions of people.
If it were only an experiment
                              I would be glad to see them try it,
but this trial will be permanent, and will erase
the past even more than wars
                              or time have been able to do.
The new order, if it is an order,
comes out of economics, as Marx foretold it
                              (as the Parthenon did not, nor the cathedrals)
                                                  —it is the culture of industrialism:
"mass production," wealth without mind
to lead it, the shape of things
obeying the laws of Smith and Ricardo (or Marx & Engels
                                    in desperate countries).
This is even apparent in Florence and Rome,
                                                                  as everywhere;
though Italy, agricultural perforce,
has been somewhat backward in beginning—
                         Rapallo is "completely changed" after ten years,
                              and here they have "fenced off" the ruins.
So that what violent politics
and the one-party system may add or take away
makes little difference, will leave no monuments.
The ruins of department stores
                              will not impress, in days to come,
as these colonnades do, nor will they stand
before the tourist with dignity and order.

65

I am sure the Italians would trade in Santa Croce
(with all the bones that are in it)
for a row of comfortable Duplex houses
on the outskirts of Montreal.
It's the one against the other. And where do we stand?
We, we are not given the choice.
We are a principle in ourselves,
a foreign body in those suburbs;
building something in the mind only, whose shape, dim
and white, trembles and becomes solid sometimes—
the one good line in a poem.

66

Rome

The present is all too present
and the past all too past:
streetcars and Roman crowds, a monstrous static
of old echoes and new noise.
I cannot hear my own heartbeat,
how should I hear what falls
from the columns of the Twelve Gods
or the hoarse whispers that grow like moss
on the stumps of the Rostra?
Rome was not built in a day, but a day is enough
once it is over, to make an end of Rome.
Nothing has power that was only power
when it lived and had its will; only the power
that is married to beauty survives. Virgil was not satisfied
with his epic when he died, nor Marc Aurelius
that he was wise.
We may learn from this how the hours should be adorned
with leaves
and the columns of days garlanded.

68

Until these letters came I had not known
how far we had gone
over the sea, the broken crags
and ruins, empty death's heads
of forgotten vigour:
hambones of the saints,
the spearholes of gladiators,
and the parched remains of St. Cecilia's hair.
But you, sweet children of light, my friends,
whose letters come by post,
are all earnest and alive,
write, asking where I am, what I have seen,
and make me know how lonely
and isolated we have been among the ruins.
The past is something one learns and contemplates
only to make the present a diamond
as hard as the Duomo of Siena,
brilliant in all facets.
To be torn from these roots is to be dying.
But I would rather have my friend's new poem
than all the Coliseum,
which is a blood-stained stable, fallen in ruin,
and your kind letters, than all the sculptured words
in all the crumbling friezes.

WHAT GREECE HAS GIVEN

69

Coming back to it all, we know it is more of a miracle
than the sea suggests:
what the Greeks did, the Italians.
"I don't know if it is because I am Greek," said
the young man on the packet,

"but the sea seems bluer,
            the sky bluer than anywhere."
A touch of nostalgia. And we know, we know
what made the Greeks a nation
of Lotos Eaters, and the Italians Sybarites
   —war, and civil war, and centuries of serfdom—
but what made them "the Greeks", we do not know.

Michael tells me
that there will be a renaissance.
But the power is in America, the new Rome.
If we could find out the secret
of these white rocks
            and hand it on to "big business"
and "the common man", America would know—
                        for 3000 years at least.
But could they ever understand it?
About virtue? The qualities of character?
Or to talk like Socrates?
The sea rinses its mouth and says nothing.
The waves act as if they did not remember.

70

We have seen bits of this marble
            scattered over all the cities of Europe:
how could it be entire? What Greece has given,
and been robbed of, was so much
          they have left nothing for themselves—
            a beggared people, cheating the tourists
on every menu, smiling insidiously,
          living now without cleanness, without order,
surrounded by deserts, the pinkish-white mountains
                parched by the sun,
that one must cross, to Delphi, to Mycenae,
to the cape over the sea at Sunion.

Time and the wars have destroyed it all, but the Acropolis
standing there, crumbling with infinite slowness,
in the sunlight,
is all that it ever was, will be, until the last speck
of the last stone is swept away by the gentle wind.
Strange, that a few fragile, chalky, incomplete blocks of marble,
worn away by time, thievery, and gunpowder,
should be enough, and all that we have come for,
to erect in the mind the buildings
of the Greeks who lived here, and their city—
akro-polis against the blue sky of heaven.
I have said of the sculptures, such people
will never again be, it is more
than we can really believe in.
Shall we ever again see such buildings? Heaven
seemed near then so that the hand could touch it.
But we have the light years,
the immeasurable solitudes.
I sit here, drinking in sunlight
from the clean candid marble,
thinking the thoughts of Plato,
of Solon, and the perfect republic.

72

The arts have been important
because their fiction worked upon
the needs of people: the Byzantine Virgin
with the sad dark boy, the great figures of athletes.
These made men understand, made them strong,
or taught them grace.
We also have suffering to deal with.
Can America learn
what Europe needs?
Learn to distrust governments and those in power . . .

Use our millions
to give the older peoples a means to live . . .
Buy the olives and currants
of Greece, the wines of France,
the dairy products of Denmark;
make those on the land self-sufficient
to keep off the rat-tooth of the ideologue
—better than tanks and artillery.
Money for schools, money for manufactures,
to keep mobs and their demagogues
from getting control in the cities.

These nations
again themselves, more or less at ease
though not up to our standard
(of living)
may begin to have time
for freedom,
for the arts, for music, the usual songs.
Now are too impoverished,
have nothing but their faces
to give us, as images of their companionable despair.

73

I do not think that we shall ever again
have great buildings. Temples and churches
built to please or placate a god
were once the occupation of a whole society
led by that superstition. The private dwelling,
or edifice of utility, no matter how pretentious
—the Pitti Palace, Chambord, Versailles—
is always an atrocity,
like a much-bejewelled dowager.

Can we find a new symbol
for all those processes
of which we are still a part?
Not until we have become perfectly accustomed
to the invention of elementary machines.

74

But we have seen the country people,
an old man and a younger,
the boy with his arm around the elder's neck,
and a spectre-thin woman with a bundle,
fragile bones under delicate skin,
dark eyed, long-suffering,
and men of fine character, with long moustaches,
quiet, thoughtful,
and women working in the fields,
the arms moving beautifully at their labour—
among the olive trees, among the grape vines,
rocky soil, dry, the farms poor and infertile,
but the people patient, inured to suffering, weather-beaten,
indifferent to the capitalist or the communist future,
to the rise or fall of cities,
arts and civilizations,
indifferent to all but the harvest, war with the soil
and the weather:
these the peasants, who come before and after.

75

And we have seen Mycenae, that old city
where Agamemnon lay buried
for 4,000 years while they were farming;
I have thought of them on these hills
when the water still flowed here,

hoeing and ploughing, breaking the rocks
patiently under the hot sun, by the road
                    once patrolled by foot-soldiers—
each stathmos still to be seen, dug in the hillside,
and the enemy always beyond in the mountains,
                                        waiting to destroy.
A clumsy city, built on a hill,
with rickety small streets climbing up to the housedoors
where the pottery stood, the water and wine jugs;
of rough-hewn stone, with simple accommodations;
but powerfully fortified against assault,
against the wars that destroy cities.
They destroyed Mycenae. And the earth covered it all,
and the walls caved in,
            which had been so carefully erected,
by slaves, of course, and the grainstores
                    filled by slaves or peasants.
It has all been excavated, to be looked at by tourists,
to be mapped and monographed
            by the French Archaeological Society.
Among the earliest of Greek cities:
                    they fought the Trojans.
Then Spartan hoplites marched over these hills,
                    over this desert,
to spoil the Athenians, to destroy Athens.
Both sides fought nobly, they say,
bringing honour to their cities.

76

That the labourer deserves to enjoy the product of his labour
is a recent discovery, unknown to history.
            It would never have crossed their minds.
But once seen and spoken, no truth of this kind
can be returned to the chaos
from which, like black diamonds, it was excavated.

There will never be art again
in any society unless it is held together by justice.
Not only that fair dealing is important
as regards the poor and ignorant peasant
who produces only the perishable
fruit, meat, and vegetables
we all consume: these and his pains
count of course in human, even animal, terms;
and love, the Christian virtue, has built cathedrals;
but justice is also important
to those above, who must deal out fairly, the bosses
who trade, who manage the state preserves.
The first beauty of all is the beauty of fair dealing
between the seller and those who buy, between the employer
and those who work.
After this, others come, in a long procession,
maidens carrying flowers, boys with branches,
cattle with hanging udders:
the marble and music
and "gold that ennobles life," *megalanora plouton*
and the flowers of song.
I have heard that there were gardens in Corinth
where one might enjoy the pleasures of the flesh
and cool water from distant mountains.
The ruins of two theatres and a temple in the Doric style
still mark the place where these pleasures were once enjoyed.

78

Even the remnant of a work of art,
like the broken temple at Delphi,
has an obvious ethical content.
I agree with Ruskin.
Not that the good can be easily defined:
there are many forms
of activity, conditions of character.

Evil is whatever denies or destroys
                    a human capability.
This temple is very beautiful
          because it is a kind of personal
record, the report of a man; one would have loved
            to live with such people.

79

The forms of beauty are many.
I liked those goats on the mountain,
the hillside covered with olive trees,
                    and the little children
playing in the villages.
          A Turkish sword-hilt, very elaborate,
and a Byzantine church filled with mosaics,
               are too a manifestation
of infinite creativity (of nature, the gods in us)
which has made our intelligence,
each particular and simple,
the everyday person we live with
who grows to flower by loving and living.

83

As for democracy, it is not just the triumph
          of superior numbers,
but that everyone, continually,
should think and speak the truth.
What freedom is there in being counted among the cattle?
The first right I want is to be a man.
It takes a little courage.
The plain truth, I say, not a few comfortable formulas
that conceal your own special lies;

the simple facts everybody knows
are so, as soon as you bring them to the light.
Democracy is this freedom, this light
shining on the human mind,
                                        light
in faces, actions—
as the Greeks once carved it in these stones.

84

By the red cliffs at Vouliagmeni
where the wind blows in from the islands,
                    from Samos, Chios, and Mytilene
no matter how filthy the land is,
the sea is clean and the wind
          cool, scrubbing the sea cliffs.
The man on the donkey is bawling "Retsina,"
the only wine they drink here,
                    a naphthaline mixture
my stomach refuses; but the grapes are "as fine as any
                    on the Italian peninsula".
Forty thousand Greeks want to go to America
                                        (said the man at the Embassy),
of these we have met a number; this land has nothing to offer.
We have seen a lot of Europe,
keeping our eyes open,
the poor villages of France, the pueblos of Spain,
                    poverty in Italy, poverty in Greece;
and England, of course, still the best corner of Europe.
It seems that we have come all this distance
to discover the virtues of America (the continent, Canada
               being a good part of it); call it a prejudice,
but minus the Coca-Cola, minus the damn advertisements,
today the land and the people
with the best working intelligence, alert and practical,
not lacking in generosity, and the will to improvement,
not lacking the social virtues;
give them an elementary education

in what makes a product permanent,
as well as useful; i.e. some sign
of the conscious life, which they have obliterated
by too much action,
as in the case of the obtuse and stupid
businessman
(one could go on with the subject),
but compared to the European
whose entire glory is in monuments
useless for the purpose of living,
the people impoverished, unpractical, uneducated,
the commercial crooks getting all that they can
out of an archaic system
(American aid going into the pockets
of bureaucrats everywhere),
the New World is every bit as good
as the immigrants imagine
(40,000 applicants,
of whom 10% will be lucky),
where wages are high and the standard of living
goes up with increasing manufacture,
where the instalment plan makes sure
you can buy some of the overproduction
(all but the military waste, all but the capital glut).
If I had my choice, I would live in Ancient Athens
first of all; but in modern Athens not at all:
40,000 Greeks have decided
that the old source of light
is the darkest place in Europe;
light moves in waves
out of the centre, to its new circumference,
whether to multi-national America
or the new barbarism of the Russians.
What new periplum
will surround the world,
war, or better, time alone, can decide.

This was written at Vouliagmeni
by the sea, the wind blowing seaward.

FINIS

85

We have come to Ithaca, Ulysses' island.
I imagine that when the hero came here
and had settled his affairs,
he was glad to have left behind
the foreign magic, foreign women,
and the long delays.
They write about Ithaca that it is "a small island
off the coast of Greece";
actually, we have already been one hour
trying to get past it.
A bigger place than one might have expected. Ulysses,
if he landed here,
would have had a good week
of hard walking to reach the end.
But this was his home. I guess he did some good
for his people (as much as in his so-called cleverness
he could)—
replenished his reserves, aided civilization—
when he got back, remembering his voyage,
remembering Troy's ruin.

86

The green hills of Italy, after the white rocks of Greece.
It was, after all, a desert:
"The farther north you go,"
said the two teachers from Lebanon,

"the more decency you'll find."
"All Greeks are dishonest," said the Greek.
But civilization travelled this way,
it's as if it had left the land behind
                    a scorched desert, exhausted
of all possibility, by so much effort.
We had travelled a long time
to get to the middle of it,
                    and now, returning
we seem to be going again
                              towards it:
"Vous avez pris le flambeau," said the Frenchman
                  speaking of America.
This circle
            has moved
                        to and from the beginning,
always going towards that
                        vanishing light.

89

In mountains, which are the white-flecked breakers
of the land, so huge the eyes become ocean-hollows,
we see what dimensions these things aspire to.
Beyond imitation. Yet whatever is essential
                                    to humanity,
is to be seen in a few mountainous endeavors—
                        a Leonardo, an Aristotle.
As in Switzerland, it is efficiency
                      which the mountains have given
for emulation: freedom, and relief from the savagery
                      of wars.
In these Alps you will find

tiny blueberries—that we picked by St. Gotthard—
                and Swiss watches,
both very excellent.
            The size of things
is not to be measured, but by the imagination.

91

We have ended as we started, looking at churches
            and Euclidean cemeteries,
from Frankfort-among-the-ruins
to the shattered face of Reims,
            an image in unstill water.
On one of the battlefields of the Marne
you picked berries
while I kicked up the nose of an exploded shell
        by the white hollow of a dugout, 1918.
The berries were good, red and sweet,
                    after 30 years,
growing among the quiet remains;
            time is trying hard to level
the trenches and shell-holes a war left behind.
Have I said enough
that wars destroy, not only the living bodies
        but all the good that men create?
Two hundred and sixty-seven shells
        fell on the Cathedral of Reims.
The Dom of Frankfort-am-Rhein
stands in a level plain, of rubble,
    where once were the fine old buildings of that city.
All Europe has been laid waste, we have seen
        what the wars have left,

from old Mycenae to new Mainz, we have seen the ruins;
little stands that we could still praise,
save cathedrals,
scarred remnants of the Europe that we came to find.

93

We ran into a heavy sea, leaving England,
fog, and unshapely waves, scythed cruelly by the wind;
the torrent passing under us then,
black, fearful,
was like a curtain suddenly; the awful ocean
closed on the continent,
blotted out Europe, the fortified walls of Cherbourg,
lights of refineries, helpless houses:
a luminous green ran under us, streaming, swirling
—I saw as in a mirror, through a manhole,
a small fishing smack tossed to and fro on the water.
Can they go on living?
The sea has washed out
everything I have written, the fiction of temporaneity:
we are back with the real, the uncreated
chaos of ocean,
which will not stop to spare us
a regret for all we have lost and forgotten.

94

Today it is cool and refreshing.
The sea is almost still,
ice-bright, hard and sun-glazed. Europe is gone.
One begins to have some perspective.
Like the dead, we remember
the symbolic events that mattered:
the red roofs of Chartres

as seen from the cathedral
where the schoolchildren sang in unison
sitting at lunch on the green; a boy we befriended in Spain
who wanted to learn from a grammar
how to speak the English tongue;
a priest on a bicycle; the Italian girls on the train
who said with their eyes that "love
is better than money"; the young man in the church
at Lancaster, and the woman who prayed
in Mainz: all these are remembered
in the first effort to return, to relive in memory
what was too little comprehended. Life, like poetry,
can only be understood through comparison, what results
is the perfect, unchanging essence,
an eidolon of the good.

95

The sea retains such images
in her ever-unchanging waves;
for all her infinite variety, and the forms,
inexhaustible, of her loves,
she is constant always in beauty,
which to us need be nothing more
than a harmony with the wave on which we move.
All ugliness is a distortion
of the lovely lines and curves
which sincerity makes out of hands
and bodies moving in air.
Beauty is ordered in nature
as the wind and sea
shape each other for pleasure; as the just
know, who learn of happiness
from the report of their own actions.

96

Incredible how the water came crashing this morning
in torrents over the bows.
Infinite, unsatisfied, the storm-driven waves
chaotically rose, sometimes culminating
by chance in such wind-shattered forms
as only the Alps or Himalayas
suggest by analogy, but vaster
because they moved, and appeared out of nowhere,
and fell massively over us.
The ship rose and fell, groaning
and crying like a kitten; all the passengers
were white again, many stayed where they had slept,
others came up just to look at the thing.
It came out of the night
and had no end. We were all helpless
before its immeasurable volume and violence.
This was certainly beauty, but of a kind not desirable
to man, who looks for happiness, and comfort
in a world he can control.
The sea in itself is more than he can take
with any real advantage.
The way for us is to keep close enough to the shore
in order to domesticate these forces,
using the sea always
to enrich our ports and inland cities.

99

And so we have arrived.
It narrows into the thin St. Lawrence.
Yet a river with a city inside it,
with a thousand islands,
as Cartier found it,
as Cabot discovered (I saw his face
in the Ducal Palace in Venice).

We have had our physical heroes,
and are also a nation
built in the middle of water.
Somehow a bigger place than we left it:
a country with certain resources,
            and a mind of its own, if lacking hunger.
The mountains of Gaspé doze, reclining,
                        in the air vacant as morning.
At home, there will be faces full of this daylight,
                  blank maybe, but beautiful.
Getting started is never easy.
We have work to do.
            Europe is behind us.
                        America before us.

6: POETRY AND TRUTH

THE PINEAL GLAND

The pineal gland, that was once an eye
on the skull's prow,
dreams now over bales of brain
behind the brow—
dreams of the sea it once knew
when it was young,
and in the darkness still as brave
rocks over thought as on a wave.

IN THIS SHINING WATCH

In this shining watch, our mechanistic universe,
whose jewels are the trembling stars,
whose casing is earth, and springs the beating brain,
we must know what time we tell in the light of day
hung in what pendulous spaces—
or the eye's glass will glisten and lose perspective,
whether looking for a needle lost in hay
or for larger regions of clockwise justice.

Knowing this, knowledge may come easier
and touch off the fighting flame;
but without it, even salvation, a new society,
is a pale land, good for ghosts,
and no one cares, or wants the ticking kingdom.

KOSMOS: THE GREEK WORLD

(For Michael Lekakis)

One day man opened his eyes and the sun blew
over his wet eyeballs a coloured flower—
kosmos of combed fields
                  and valleys where cattle grazed:
the hills folded in equations, and streams
bubbled mathematically to the sea; even the sea
strident, went silent,
            counted to ten and reined in;
and thunder gulped its peal.
            What memory of pain
he then denied, fought, shut his eyes to,
            or reconciled,
to make that intellectual gain! But he did.
It may be he mastered himself just then; or maybe
it was the blue Mediterranean dazed him
to think death is gay.
            Yet he found everything to praise.
God rose on the face of the waters I think that day
and smiled, his first recognition to clay.

TO AN UNKNOWN IN A RESTAURANT

Thank you for sitting,
though the picture I have made of you
            will not be an action
but a meditation, like frost on a window.
You have been very obliging, and patient,
not only to me, but to everyone, the world;
            therefore I will not think of you
with a gun to your temple, nor crying out
like Philoctetes, but make you the lonely figure
            in a meditative portrait,

almost lost in your background—not the sufferer
who wakes up to find he has been crucified, but like those
caged animals, born in captivity, who do not know
          why they are unhappy.

AUTUMN

Now that leaves have the falling sickness
      And poets complain of dying,
Who can deny that in the earth and air
      Something is languishing, sighing?

Lord of the Lyre pulls at the strings,
      Cassandra combs out her hair,
But Daphne droops in the laurel bough
      And Syrinx is yellow everywhere.

The marrow cools in the fatted boys
      And girls who slept under hoarding;
Policemen walk slowly and expect
      Nothing but paper and old boarding.

All die, they fall apart, lose concert,
      Because the lovers have broken
Thigh from thigh, and like a magnet
      Drop the leaves wet and soaken.

I gaze at this with an eye unbelieving
      And bitter at their proof;
I am not ready yet for grieving,
      Nor leaving, nor the funeral stuff.

The season fades all who comply,
      And they shall find their colour
In the stained yellow of the tomb;
      Or live, and deny, to suffer more.

LINES FOR P.J.W.

Amid the mind's extensions, pain
pierces a pinprick to as wide
a field as joy: all crucifixions
incarnate, all paradises gained.

You said, 'the tragedy is still one's own,
it does not help that others suffer;
suffering is tiny, unphilosophical, one's own'.
You did not add that a miniature stage

contains the world, as one, as a poem, does.
And if all things are conceptions, shadow-stuff,
who more than sufferers can conceive
the universe between this ache and that laugh?

Though only shadowy sensation makes
the moment quiver—'Plato!' I have cried,
'all that we have is appearances! . . .
But in that narrow light, *we see.*'

A WINTER SONG

Desire has gone into his winter quarters
and all those other rioters that kept him company:
pleasures of meat and drink, sweat of wrestling,
dancing, keeping late hours, getting drunk;
those companions are scattered over the plains,
eat dry crusts, crack joints, read late, drink alone.

Old Desire has gone into his winter home
and all those young bucks, who used to keep him gay:
as the sun's pleasures, and all the greenery
of the abundant grasses where one lay
in an aproned lap; the pleasure of fingers
touching, and loving by a midnight flame.

King Desire has gone into his winter sleep
taking with him the revellers that made him brave:
rhythmic rounds rapped out in repeating praise,
the breath light with love, or heavy with delays;
the wave and the wind, delight beating the body,
that blew warm words upon a woman's face.

GOLDEN HANDS

Day in a blue kimono sauntered along the sky
When you on a slice of rainbow came singing by,
Ten pizzicatti on an E-string were your hands:
Death could not reach me in your ultra-violet arms.

Blackbirds have cawed you home since, and the snake
Chased you from perch to perch on the embittered
lake,
Here I have scraped the moon with salt-white hands
And collared pearls in the oysters of both palms.

To heaven's sleepless thunder down the sultry west
The sun has dropped, a Phoenix to her nest;
Blind bats and a foghorn beat their hands,
The moon in a hoop of circles mounts a cloud.

They turn in an iron order, chariots over knives—
When shall we sleep both under dandelion lives?
I with a tongue of silver, you with your golden hands,
Will trouble no worm with a whisper when death is
loud.

KEEWAYDIN POEMS

1

The mind, a bruised element, comes to nature
to swell slowly among the trees.

Rest, rest, but there is no rest.

The unwashed city in my bones was bathed
in the 3 o'clock heat, burst, a black scorpion,
and then the water
rinsed off the acid and the hell ticks.

Now I am tired but clean.

Have seen the poplar leaves playing Chopin
without crescendo
and the sky stopped behind them,
boring but beautiful.

Is there anything in this I may have missed?
The same picture will be there tomorrow.

2

Today the sky began to move.
That is what I do not understand.
Our mental habits proceed:
curse, piss, wash, eat hash,
is all very good, but not
very different from the past,
not very true, not close to 'it',
real but not 'real', no flash
of paradigmatic insight comes of it.
Layton says 'you missed', Currie sneers,
the wind blows the leaves like yesterday,
God has not spoken, but that's okay,

I register the same old feelings
in the same familiar way:
the mole's in his lair, the insects hiss
as they cut the 'symbol-extricating' air.
I have already formed the habit
of sitting on a rock as on a chair.
And the clouds move, they move.
I do not understand. That's why
I've grown accustomed not to ask them why.

3

What we call nature is nothing else than
the triumph of life other than our own—
the passive unaggressive trees
and the grass, so alien
they can have no animal contact with us
and are therefore safe
to walk through—they and the inert
inanimate—
a world huge and useless, from our point of view,
therefore a bore
(i.e., if you've got something else to do
that you're glad to do),
or a place for free association,
for God the Father, Mother Nature,
and 'our sister water'—
the friendly family (we like to think) of things alive;
or better still, that beneficent 'other',
a great deal of 'not mankind',
hence at least a counterweight to human ego—
but most of all, a place of freedom, to ruminate in, to be
forever blowing bubbles
of so-called 'relaxation',
for fantasy that has not already found its images
of successful art, in living.
But do not say that it brings you
closer to the unity of any process
that we may be a part of,

or that to pile on enough vegetables
            and rocks
is the epiphany of philosophy.

4

Yet green is a pleasure to live with,
            among the colours
a kind of world
of straw, on sticks, stirring yet stationary—
the comic vegetation hung out in rags, flags,
            piled in barrows of bushes—
                  like a Victorian parlor
in which there is still room
for you, if you don't mind stepping over the bodies
growing and dying, gasping for air,
if you, indifferent to murder
            in forms of life not our own,
love the world we live in—
haletant with genocide and innocent abominations
            and all the green pleasures.
We need to think of nothing but ourselves,
and it is so. Which we do.
The order of things, everywhere,
takes care of that also:
relax, kill and live.

5

So man, the top killer of them all,
who has brought three-quarters of the birds, fish, and animals
close to extinction
and now does his slaughtering systematically
            (all save man-killing war, murder, and sport,
            which still take the natural form),
persists in the Western-Christian idea,
the romantic theory of nature:
            that order rules,
            that love governs.

6

For tenderness is also a principle,
        the best in our sad experience,
and we would have it all, all tenderness—
as every woman would be a nymph,
all poems about love,
all men lotos-eaters—
        a perpetual sipping of emotional whipping-cream.
So the sentimentalist,
the tearful convert, the nun,
the child, and the young bourgeoise mother,
        all for whom tough living is done by somebody else.
Violence is self-regarding, to say the least,
but tenderness is not: this
        the condition of our existence cannot too much afford.
Therefore all virile (beautiful) action is driven by these
        in turn, or in a manly association
(the she-cat licking her young,
        gentle, but not self-indulgent):
the male and the female principle—let's hope
        that each of us has a strain of both
(and here is my hail and farewell
        to the twisty-sexed—
may they suffer less, and meet their own kind!)
But where all is reconciled, power sleeps
        in the atoms of heaven.
O death, keep for me that lock which binds love and cruelty,
and now I will suffer them apart, in silence!

7

The kosmos, it was man created the kosmos.
The chaos was there, but man created the kosmos.
The world I see (this poem)
I make out of the fragments of my pain
and out of the pleasures of my trembling senses.
Not all have, or see the same.
Like a cock on a dunghill,
        because there are worms,

out of my desires I make a world to be loved.
Beyond this, I do not know.
Beyond this, tears for the human state.

8

Now these trees are like no other splendor.
The aesthetic shape that water and sky have
beats the skyscraper,
because the carnal tragedies are resolved there
in more satisfactory proportions
        (especially at sunset,
        if you know what I mean).
But unfortunately we cannot live here;
like poetry, know only that it exists
—and to have created the idea
        is good as to have made the world—
a single vision to contain
death and the other fragments.

9

And it is to enjoy, simply to enjoy.
Now the water fretting the wharf gently,
        the wind teasing the water,
now the flies colliding in their love action.
The sun makes me dizzy, but I am not unaware
        of how her lines compose;
or how my love tempts me and yet refuses;
and how my dozing consciousness
        throbs into life again and grows.
I am not unlike the world around me,
many and muddled, a contradictory thing,
yet like the lake water, swell with some clear
        delicious spring . . .
                Shall I stand up and crow?

And shall I ever understand
all that the spaniel senses know?
Sing, swallows, and touch the horizontal water!
Cry, loon, tonight on the cold, cold lake.
I am prepared to take in my falling fever
with a convalescent's appetite
all your sweet delights and agonizing screams.

DIRTY STUFF

After the love affair in the white bed
she left her stool somehow
in the white bowl: I looked at it with terror,
brushing my teeth and spitting into the sink.
It washed down to a satanic sound
as if all hell were roaring at
our love.

'You're full of shit,' the ordinary expression,
is a statement of horrifying fact:
the gut meandering through the body
and the blood-stream collecting smells
to be expelled by the arse;
when you think of it,
high culture is a matter of saying things like that neatly;
the *ars poetica*,
how to enjoy relief by understatement.

How stupid our forefathers were!
Judge, by how vulgar I must be
to make my meaning clear.
But what if they had never drawn the line?

Nature draws it—
my cat covers his bit.
But eats it, off his own behind.
It's no use learning from cats.
'Human nature' is mostly
our unnatural habits; but if what we might have been
is a futile question, what we might be is not.
The excesses of 'the finer sense' make love too difficult
and leave to hate
all the weapons of plain fact.
Religion, poetry, and love
are shot away by petards . . .
which we could answer with, if we had them in our arts.

So there's my love lying on her white pillow
and here the noise trying to wash away
the poem with her sewage.

PROVINCETOWN

I. RESORT CENTER

The problem
          was to reconcile the public beaches
               with the veritable Atlantic:
as in 'Europe',
          the tourists
scattered on the sand,
against the rock-scalloping water;
we among them, as you said,
          'the town gets the better of us'.
But does the Atlantic,
          ever to be remembered?
for which we go to the lonely places
and the empty beaches
          (whatever they touch
is like them, these multi-arseholed
          mass-mindless Americans—
          because they've been here, the sand is filthy the ocean
               trivial)
Or try to think of gales
as the old thing throws you,
think of breaking a continent,
and the sheets of water that heaped these sands up,
in fine, what dignity there is in a sculpted shell
          and the dune grasses . . .
But for man, in a jockey cap,
eating Tastee-Freez
by a shore of beer-cans and wax-paper—
          nothing but shame,
a wave of impotent anger, and silence.

2. ART COLONY

To be an artist in America is almost compulsory,
for the few who resist it,
            the garboil of democracy,
and want to prove their difference
by the only true excellence—
            in art, not art-work;
having nothing to do with all this,
only expectorate and say ———
            (calling a spade a spade)
or like the Saturday Evening Post, or the ads,
treat it with Southern romanticism:
the family picnic, with the old Ford car
            now a new Buick,
the Heinz Ketchup and Coca-Cola;
but the superior caste eschew
either alternative, in their pure poetry
            of abstraction,
the signals of personal superiority, god help them,
and hell take them—
to the expensive galleries: the rich will pay,
having the same motives
            as artists
                        to be apart from the crowd.
But all that's too pure to be poetry,
because art is not that clean.
                (O beautiful feather
fallen from a seagull's wing,
you smell of the elements and the sweet society
                where you belong!)

3. FISHING VILLAGE

And then the old inhabitants,
        kind,
or bigoted, after their kind,
stick-to-itive as grass—Acadians, Portuguese, English—
who built the white town
now placarded with whimsical art-work
        (not art),
the gentry, wrinkled with work
        on the white whittling foam
and their descendants
        and ladies of the land:
the bent little old one, who made a meticulous point
        of not overcharging
(the Fathers at this would have been cheered,
but not by the gin bottles
        lying on the bank,
nor by the beauties walking the streets . . .)
So the shaping spirit of work
                 can make a town;
but we have made all of our world
        with our own machines,
and now the unnatural man
must come to the plain old town, to see how it was,
quiet and quaint old streets
        and honest people,
from whom he can learn less than nothing—
        not even the good manners
to bathe himself and leave the ocean clean.

4. NEWS

He fell from the roof
of the dock-shed onto the wharf
hitting it with his knees—
one of the boys
diving all day into the deep water
and climbing on odd corners, to do it,
I saw him
lying on the fish-cart,
his legs tied up in a towel,
and his arms terribly shaking, the eyes closed.
It comes like that
some little accident to prove
the genial power over us
that death preserves:
the mourning sister so beautiful,
the silent bathers,
and the pale lips of the boy.
The ocean cannot come near to it in magnificence,
nor can we degrade it
by using it for our pleasure.

5. THE OCEAN

But when the water roars around us
and the sky bellows,
the sea-birds mewing
falling upon the minnows,
the seagulls resting against the wind
and the small scallops, the crabs, the
crustaceans
heaving and falling, torn upon the tide
rolling in,
that gives them its shape, of a tiara,
or a chandelier of jelly,
a groping claw—
I think of man,
prone under striped umbrellas
and oily with lotions,
who has outdone the speed of the mackerel
and the sea robin,
has filed the tooth of the tiger
and made a fiber of sharkskin: the winner,
the wordy vanquisher
of the streaming kingdoms,
of the armored, the swift, and sharp-clawed—
man in a bathing suit,
looking out over the ocean.

6. AVANT GARDE

We can't give them up, though,
the middle classes
of new America.
In Provincetown, home of the Fathers,
coming to meet the old
out on a sand bar
in the steps of the Pilgrims
to the first sweet water,
on the barbs of whalers;
knobby in knickers, they talk to each other,
looking at relics:
'What does it prove?'
'That it's shock-proof and water-proof'
(a watch in a window);
but somewhere the area
of difference widens
(the old and the new)
enough for an ocean,
and children go dizzy
seeing their fathers
astride on a yew tree—
ridiculous posture!
They, like the fisherman,
spit with the wind now,
and what all the artists
know, they won't stoop to tell you.

Look, how the birds
are diving against each other!
Almost, the curved wave catches them.
That's how we are, in the void,
between the now and hereafter!

'Good morning, Mr. Greenpepper.'

THE SEA AT MONHEGAN

Torrent and torment, the ocean's revel
of spawning and eating
the spit of one another, rocky toothsome scarabs,
stinking sea-kelp, barnacles and scales—

out of which the white reef,
sea-gull, tuna,

the eye, and the delicate reaching heart's
                    anemone.

Its designation, like wing marks or fins
or the manyshapes of the marine flora:
a mind—to hurt, or amuse
with skies, seascapes, truths!

Then lost in that great indifference
(as it is a great concern)
our fitful lives on this volcanic island,

a living green in mid-ocean,
a lick of the too-great energy,

that these hills in their sequences, swells,
wrap and fold, nurse to their mother rhythms.

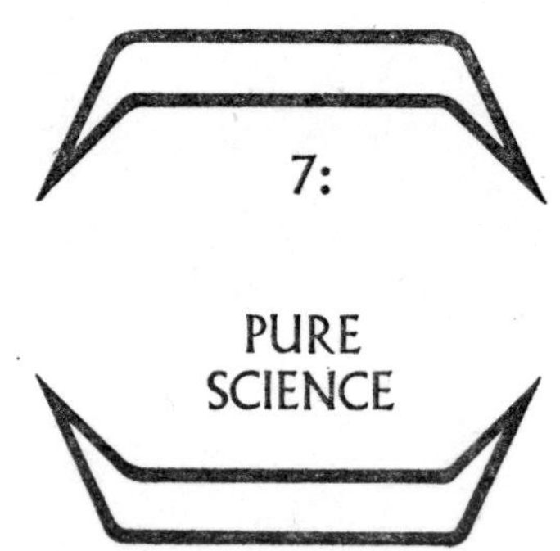

7: PURE SCIENCE

PURE SCIENCE

Poetry is a man-made kite
skating on an imaginary sky,
But nobody knows what the sky is
nor why there are kite-makers.

It is also like grandmother's idea of heaven
that we have learned to do without
Because nobody cooks there,
sleeps with girls, or mints money.

It is a whirling
spark in a vacuum,
And only scientists seem to
enjoy the experiment.

FAIR CALYPSO

Love came like a midnight fever
And went away—
night wind with the dawn.

Now the days are quiet
islands in a dark sea.

Tell me,
where is that storm?
Where is the wave that carried me
to her side?

AN AIR BY SAMMARTINI

It was something you did not know
          had existed—by a dead Italian.
Neither words nor a shape of flesh
          but of air;
                    whose love it celebrated
                    and "cold passion"
Amoroso Canto, a crystal
          that fell from musical fingers—
As a cloud comes into the eye's arena,
          a certain new tree
                    where the road turns,
          or love, or a child is born,
                    or death comes:
Whatever is found or is done
          that cannot be lost or changed.

FLOWER SONG

All I got out of you was a cactus,
but even that, from you, was okay.
It stands now in my window;
I am sad because you have gone away.

It has rained almost every day since you left.
It rained when you went, rained more after.
Wet newspapers in the streets, the days cold,
and the nights without laughter.

I am sitting now thinking of how you went about singing
and never worried;
for you were never anything but gay. You gave me
only a cactus. And yet today
I listened to your soundless violin
in an empty corridor.

A SHORT SPEECH

Because they do not last,
are they less a delight?
A lifetime itself is not a very long time,
and not a work of art either;
but who would turn from it, the living of it,
on that account?
We hang on as long as we can
and hate to think how quick it flies.
And as for art, that's very long
—at least we used to think so,
yet Chaucer says
'al shal passe that men prose or ryme,
take every man his turn, as for his tyme. . .'
And where are Sappho's best
short-lived lines? Where are Abelard's songs?
What is most like true art
looks as if it might not last,
looks as high and split-second beautiful
as that quiver of your lips was. . .
And then, maybe it will last forever, who knows?

DIVINE TOUCHES

Toiling with the white smoke of your body,
wreathed in the dark smoke of carnality,
I was whirled and turned into a feather of poppy
sleepily floating over distant people.
Now awake and alone
I walk in the rain-soft night
borne still on that contemplation.
We become selfless by common living,
drowned in loud vision or in sound,
but what we are alone, or in love, is the risen self
that gains from every birth or death
and walks out over the corpse of the flesh.

OLD SONG

Since nothing so much is
as the present kiss
don't let an old kiss
so disconcert you,
but know it is no crime
to give a new kiss time
and reason to convert you.

The first you ever had
was an eternal lad
whose smile was very May
no other mouth replaces,
but this today
has an October way
to harvest his embraces.

Loves are the fruits of time
different and the same
the perfect and imperfect,
and in the body's branches
where old kisses hang
and sweet birds sang
the wind fills his paunches.

And any kiss at all
is present after all
for now is all we have
now when we want them,
so grant your kisses leave
to give and to receive
nor waste your lips to count them.

THE JACKPOT

Beauty beauty beauty.
Does an old woman *have* to be beautiful
            for the old man to love her
Or the paper flowers she carries
            a work of art?
What *you* want is not luck,
            nature's jackpot,
but an intellectual seal of order and approval.
But pleasure overflows, and love
            overflows, and beauty overflows!

SONG WITHOUT TEARS

Do you shed tears for the dead
      When you do read them?
And is it just that being read
      They do not need them?

Each time they say, 'I must die!'
      Do you think, 'so he has'?
No, it isn't the dead at all
      Who must die, alas!

But we, who are still quite warm,
      Nor yet 'immortal',
Who repeat what the others said
      When they were mortal.

R.I.P.

How do you think we'll rest
With tombstones on our chest?
I had rather recline
With your breast on mine,
        Love, on violets.

Or how shall we know peace
Broken piece by piece
In decay? I'd rather fret
Now for what I get
        From lips like these,

And leave nothing to wish
When we've become a dish
For the worms, my friend.
Leave them, hot heart, at end
        Cold cuts to finish.

THE FOLLY

Strange that, having thought you were through to despair,
now love can shake what remains and bother
someone you had rather walk with and talk to
than sleep all night with any other.

Confess this fiction a middle-ageing folly,
and this love now, for a sad lady,
desire to find a like and to recapture
joy with her that you might make her gay

and beautiful as she is, as you would be!
Love had always a self-cheating twist
like those poems you cannot help but make;
and age makes one love, as youth did, a mist.

But still we will love until the end,
—love while women are made of clay,
with those sad features lonely for God
and the body crumbling into decay.

FORESIGHT

When I have carded the wool of your thoughts
and found the physiological knot
from which your terrors proceed which make you *you*,

and we have opened the electric lock
together, and entered the current of desire,
we shall know the rock on which each of us was broken:

as personal pain, impersonal politics,
meet in that immediate knowledge
where none is alone, yet each torn and separate,

the chain gang, the refugee enclosure,
so we shall know what makes ourselves
part of a world, moaning without a doctor.

INTERPRETATION OF DREAMS

Plagued by the ills of aching memory
I remembered the libido-theory of Freud,
how the unsatisfied neural tremors
wrangle with the ego out of key.

Since then, our two bodies have tuned
in that concert music for mixed instruments
which drowns the dim grating echoes
of a personal agony in a room;

and it's good to think that, for the time,
you have replaced the other scrapings,
for when I think of any of them
my tongue stumbles thrumming your name.

A CRACKER JACK

If you and I ceased to exist, my dear,
 and all other ghosts,
would the Manifold of Space and Time
 collapse in its cupboards?

Would the quivering fiction of being
 Joe, Paul, Patsy, May
be folded up like their Snakes and Ladders
 and be laid away?

As if we had not been? Not only 'as if'
 but as it is.
Nature destroys itself: we are and are not.
 Are now like this,

then never have been, when we cannot remember
 and no one is there to see
where shadfly swarms go after rainstorms
 or flies in a laboratory.

Our summer of strongest sunlight recalls
 the greatest sadness;
and the quiet contemplation of our extinction
 is called beauty, dearest.

NO ANSWER

A woodpecker knocked on my skeleton
    And found it very hollow
        And very thin
    Where all my aching marrow
        And blood had been.
Then he gave a rap and hopped
    To the crown at the top.

'Knock-knock! Who's there?' he spelled.
    'Tis I,' my soul replied.
        Then he with skill
    Hopped down and looked inside,
        Cleaning his bill
On my nose (or where it once was)
        With a wink and a pause.

'Ho ho!' said he. 'What's this? Are you there?'
    He cocked his head and clicked.
        'How's tricks, mon cher?
    I see you've been cleaned and picked
        Something rare.
But can you hear it still in that box
    When your knees knock?

Ha ha!—in that box, when your knees knock!'
    I looked at him through my jaws
        And my empty eye,
    And got angry, and I was
        About to reply—
When he saw an apple tree
    And whistled away.

WHEN YOU DENIED ME

When you denied me, I was mad
            with spiritual love—
seeking in your body my cure.
You granted what I desired
and love declined.

Then because you did not love me
I was still mad with hot sex.
            You said you loved me:
both my lust and my love died.

As active passion, active love,
now they coexist, tempering
            each other's excess.

THE PERFECT LOVERS

The good you do me, love,
is being like no other I ever dreamed of,
so real, all others were dreams of you.

Beauty, reality, the sex we desire
become unlike in our mating bodies
what they were, and seem to be creative

by their accord, as are the parts of nature
when they marry and make in delight
—fire, or flowers.

We love, but do not understand
how our meeting is privileged and more perfect
than any fact, of love or trade.

MARRIAGE

Something in man delights
        in order and kindliness
        though the gods deny him.
Our fingers touching say this
        and the children sleeping
        in your untouched loins.

Tomorrow we join in marriage
        with ring and sweet song
        and the tears of the old.
When we die our dusts scatter;
        but where we have loved so
        no gods need recall.

MARCH WIND

It'll take just such a madman as you
to loosen up the starch of reason
        that's gripping the world in cold formality.
But when you sweep the ivory canes
and the stiff shirt from the house corner
and smash the monocle on the backyard puddle,
        you'll still have the people, chilled in propriety,
to prod with some up-the-petticoat obscenity
        before we can go on
        to meet the lascivious summer.

8: LAUGHING STALKS

TO THE READER

All right, all right,
          so I write too much!
But I can't say for you, dear reader,
          that you read too much.

THE LAYMAN TURNED CRITIC

Seeing an elephant, he sighed with bliss:
"What a wonderful nightingale this is!"

And of a mosquito he observed with a laugh,
"What a curious thing is this giraffe."

POETRY FOR INTELLECTUALS

If you say in a poem "grass is green,"
They all ask, "What did you mean?"

"That Nature is ignorant," you reply;
"On a deeper 'level'—youth must die."

If you say in a poem "grass is red,"
They understand what you have said.

M

TO BEAT THE RACKET

After they have all decided
that you are a strictly personal poet,
write nothing about yourself
for the next ten years;
and then when they say you lack consistency
                    of development,
write an imposing literary essay
in which you make the point
that some "unapparent consistency"
is the hallmark of "generative virtue"
and some friendly critic
will appear
very soon after.
And when they say you are among the great
of a *past* generation,
write something under a pseudonym
and let them discover you.

THE CURE

When I was young I used to lie
To every maiden that I met,
Saying, "I love you . . . and I sweat
Past midnight, all because of you;"
But all night long snored like a dog
Tired of hunting—you know what.

Now older, kinder, lying less,
I whistle through the day as free
As any dog who's had his day,
And say I do not love at all;
But all night long I often sweat
Thinking of what I would forget.

BIOLOGY FOR SCHOOLS

The birds and the bees
Do as they please;
Kittens and dogs
Do it, and hogs
Never refuse;
By four and by twos
Hippos go to it;
Hawks in mid-air
Have an affair;
Ducks in a pond
Always respond;
In oceans the whales,
On grasses the snails;
Bugs in the moon,
Germs in spittoons;
In a lover's rose
Or a dead man's nose
Worms do it; and fish
In a glass or a dish
Do it at their ease
Whenever they please.

In dung, the annelida,
On mountains the felidae;
On ashes the cricket,
The deer in a thicket;
In fire the Phoenix,
The virus on Kleenex:
Without any fuss
All of them just
Do as they please—
The he's with the she's.
Noiseless or loud,
Humble or proud,
In flocks and in herds,
In schools (mark the words),
In private, in company,

With or without any
Limits of season,
Restraint, rhyme or reason,
Do with abandon
What instincts demand and
Occasion permits—
They do it, and quits.

But man, when he reaches
Manhood and breeches,
Does nothing like these
Birds, insects, and bees
When he meets with the she's
Biological features.
This lord of the creatures
With reason accursed
Must think of it first,
Must think well and long
Of right and of wrong,
Must ask for permission,
First of the wished one,
Then parents and priests,
Of two friends at least,
Of psychologists, breeders,
Perhaps teacup readers;
Must ask his employers,
Doctors and lawyers—
And even, in hope,
May petition the Pope.

At last, if he's told
He may have and hold,
He is ready to hurtle
The weeks to the fertil-
ization he's panted
For three years at least
To accomplish, as beast.
Everything granted,
The moment draws near:
He readies his gear,

A silk hat and tails,
A ring . . . how he quails!
Then in a church
He goes with a lurch,
Walks down an aisle
To pray for his trial;
Then seals with a pact
The terrible act,
Taking oath he will never
After this, ever,
Do with another
What he's done with such bother.
If he does, there is hell . . .

But there goes the bell!

We've learned this, at least:
Between man and beasts
There's a difference—it teaches
They practice, he preaches.

PSYCHOANALYSIS

Having slept with him for three years
She feels now that he is not going to ask her
To marry him; so she has begun to "go out"
With somebody else.

This makes him very unhappy.
He wonders now whether he still 'loves her"
Enough to want her back.
He is "working this out" with his analyst.

SUNDAY PROMENADE

Out for my Sunday walk
I've had a vision, Jock,
That's going to make you smile
At your Spengler and Carlyle!

It was a trail of mothers
With 10,000,000,000 bloody bothers
Toddling in their tracks
Through the city parks:
Whale-sized madonnas
With their tiny Jonahs,
Skinny mam'selles
Nursing teapot hells;
Exasperated mammas,
Pesky little yammerers,
Dumpy, ruddy marms
With copies in their arms.
Bawling at their brats,
Cleaning up their slats,
Slapping little asses,
Wiping snot in masses,
While the billion dears
Messing in their rears
Or leaking at the nose,
Oozing at their mouths,
Were scraping in the sands
With sucker-sticky hands:
Savage young missies,
Shrieking girls and sissies,
Bawling kids in jumpers,
Tots in baggy rompers,
Tots in bulging bloomers
(Heavy, thick, and numerous).
Boys with knees in plasters
(Noisy little bastards).
All with grabbing manners,
All with nagging mammas;

And all of them could squall
For a rocker, stick, or ball.
But suddenly in the stench
Of infant Untermensch,
I saw in each small bum
A double world-to-come . . .
It was a vision, Jock,
To beat the atomic shock!
Markets full of mouths,
Consumers massed in crowds,
Diapers full of jazz,
Comics, TeeVee, Ads,
Future baseball fans
Holding in their hands
Soapsuds, Toothpaste, News—
Everything by twos.
I saw the Total Chaos
That's rising to destroy us:
A monster in swaddling bands
With 10,000,000,000 eyes and hands.

The Thing is coming, Jock.
We're in for a stinking shock!

PARODIES OF CANADIAN POETS

PROEM

If anyone should take offense
the poet can only say:
    I am not responsible.
    If I killed anyone
    It was only in play.

JAMES REANEY'S DREAM INSIDE A DREAM, OR THE FREUDIAN WISH

I dreamed that my grandmother
gave birth to a grandfather clock
and out of the clock came my grandfather
and in his hand was my jock;
and I awoke out of this dream
and dreamed I was putting on my sock
when out of the sock came my grandmother
holding my grandfather's jock;
and I awoke out of this dream
and found myself in my socks
under the grandfather clock,
and in my hand was *my* jock.

PROF. BIRNEY'S LECTURE

This is a grade school land
Stuck in the three R's:
Rigmarole, Romanticism, and Commarse.
What shall we do about this state of affairs?
Shall we grow up?
Consider, father's gone to the Blind Pig,
Mother's in bed with a cold.
Uncle (with the glass eye) has kicked the bucket
Without leaving any of us a cent.
Gonorrhoea not excluded—
Can we learn before it's too late?
Take out your Anglo-Saxon grammars, boys,
And repeat after me:
HWAET WE GARDENA IN GEARDAGUM. . . .

A SCRAP FROM A. J. M. SMITH'S NOTEBOOK

O (ah) to write one poem
as crisp and pure as the ice
in this Great Canadian Frigidaire

where my intense and passionate
soul, laid bare,
would become one . . . intense and passionate prayer . . . (?)
. . . ? . . .

IRVING LAYTON'S POEM IN EARLY SPRING

My friends, the people are devouring each other.
They will finish me off soon
with a gorpeous icepick.

They are mephitic as fly dung on cherry-stones.

But these pregnant buds opening like your
genitals
Are beautiful, dear, and swollen with greatness
Like my poems.

SWITCHBOARD OPERATORS
(P. K. Page)

From Monday through Friday (if not on the
bivouac on Sunday)
they practice their pistils upon honeyless combs,
are frayed, are frigid, combining their hair-do's
of wire Medusa, wearying at boxes of Pandora
and pain; and they are eavesdroppers,
are message collectors; are, in spite of
feasts of hisses and yeasts of ho,
comely to all comrades, with fingers for tresses;
are voices to some, are noises; are mouths
for meeting, not kissing, eating an imaginary crumpet.

RICH MAN'S PARADISE
(After F. R. Scott)

Behold these happy children at the Laurentian spa
Playing the juke box and drinking Coca-Cola:
Yet they must return to Lagauchetière Street
After this little treat
To waste their stunted, unprofitable lives
For the profit of the few, under what we persist in calling
"The System of Free Enterprise"!

SOUSTER'S LAMENT

The beer was fine, the long green bottles on the table,
The lights were dim, the rhythm of the band just right,
The floorshow was just over, the girls gone for a
 quick one upstairs—
I wondered, what will they have in store for me—
When I said to myself, how long can you go on kidding
 yourself
About the beer, and the whores, and the Men's Room behind you?
But we went on drinking, because there were still two
 bottles left
And we had aching hearts, and had lips.

QUEBEC RELIGIOUS HOSPITAL

by A. M. Klein

Scarp Aesculapian, promontorious embole,
Refluct and invert of populous teleopaths,
My youth's diagony, jejeune floraison,
I bow to you crutchless, in memory's name . . .
(unfinished)

CARMAN'S LAST HOME

In "Sunshine House" lived Mrs. King
Where Carman with a turquoise ring
Dangled the bell, and often stayed,
Talked and sang, and wept and prayed.

At "Moonshine" on a summer's day
They danced in sandals—the Delsarte way—
while Unitrinian silence made
Their sorrows one, their joys a shade.

In "Ghost House" stayed eternal Bliss,
Melancholy, despite all this;
Sang of pure Love, and the Mystic One,
Wore his hair long, his tie undone.

They have passed on, and "Sunshine" too,
As all great luminaries do:
A Ryerson Chapbook contains the man
Of Vagabondia and the Pipes of Pan.

LAMPMAN

"He had a horror of stuffed birds," (that's news);
Loved Nature, though; took long walks, still.
Hated his job, loathed Parliament Hill;
But wrote about what seasons fit the Muse.

A Socialist, a Fabian, Feminist,
A critic of "false coin"—Commerce, and Wealth—
He sat in his corner, at a desk, to sweat
Over "David and Abigail," "The Organist".

The Ineffable, the Invisible, tempted him,
Although he'd rather a cold, prosaic eye
(Formula: To praise—yours not to reason why);
Too many "stuffed birds", then, too little vim.

The best solution to emerge, of course,
Was "apartment houses, delicatessen stores."

HELLCATS IN HEAVEN

(Report on the book *Cerberus*)

François Villon read one half,
Ended with a bitter laugh:
"May you be hanged for this,"
He said. "It's awful stuff!"

Next to read was William Blake,
Said in a fit of coughing shakes:
"Will you build Jerusalem
With the boards of a jakes?"

Read it then, Arthur Rimbaud,
Read it shuddering as though
He had tasted something foul;
Then bawled, "Merde—ça pue!"

Read it Maitre Rabelais,
Laughed, but fell a-cursing too:
" 'Tis true I said *faictz ce que veut*—
But how could I know what you would do?"

TAR AND FEATHERS

Layton, we write our clabbered verses,
Yours a long catalogue of curses,
Mine one pure curse the song traverses—
And yet the fact's we both know what
We're cursing isn't worth a futt.
Old Ez advises "build a sewer"
When culture's gone into manure;
Mistaking his advice at times
We make a sewer of our rhymes.
Of course, the Montrealers' lives
Are dismal—they deserve their wives—
Of course the poems in the *Star*
Are worse than yours and mine, by far.
And Westmount's cultured smell is spoil
Refined from Point St. Charles's oil.
Sure what they read and what they think,
And say, gives off an awful stink.
The soda fountain "five-foot shelf"
Would have choked Gutenberg himself;
The stomach turns from what they feed
Their young, like sparrows, true indeed,
And yet, we itch to double-kill
What there is left half-living still.
Think of the mountain how it stands
And doesn't give a damn what cans,
Cupcakes and condoms people throw
Over its calm Shakespearean brow.
There will be time yet, mountains think,
To wash all cities down the sink.
That's how I'd like to stand at last,
If lust or inspiration last.
Here by the Fount of Youth, it's warm,
Coffee and pie need no reform,
The waitress makes quick verses come.
Teenagers crowd around the rack
Of sex and crime, but stay intact.
To pin-ball magic eyeballs roll,

The Farmby Program fills the soul,
Telling the folks how many cows
Were burned last night while chewing chows,
Who had a birthday, who ate hash
And died of piles in St. Eustache. . .
And shall we curse the cook who makes
The pink floss on the Pom-Pom cakes?
Or bend to mop the floor with poems
They'll hang to drip in all good homes?
Such choices still defeat our ends;
It's waste of time that passion spends,
For dead men all know something worse
Than still to be alive to curse!
The young are coming, whistling songs
And we shall go like dinner gongs,
But Montreal will have its fleas
Though what you write "to teach and please"
Is swelling notes for Ph.D.'s.

The waitress asks me, "Something else, sir?"
"No, thanks." For once, no Bromo Seltzer.

THEY'RE WONDERFUL

But it's a lot of horseshit this
stuff of yours you call
poetry Why don't you guys talk straight
I know you're
fakers because
I've seen you and you look like fakers
You squeal and squirm if
somebody says christ this stuff stinks
All of you are
in the ash-can frankly You
haven't got a thing to say to anybody

I've looked into your
chap—
books and frankly I am dis—
gusted with
your la-de-da Why don't you guys make French pastry
Why don't you play chess It's just as good
for your speed Or why don't you get
yourself a piece instead of making these bits
I tell you fellas it isn't
worth it Your stuff is just
a joke You haven't got a thing I'm sorry
for you Really fellas I'm sorry
for you poets You get as pale as
macaroni reading and
writing doodads
when you're missing such a hell of a lot
You're missing a lifetime buddies
Come on out and have a glass of
beer and see
what there is to see Look at these bee-utiful
asses in the street
Try a hot-dog Give it a lot of
relish And take off your glasses What
you like this eh It's noisy but
not so bad when they're changing
records Yeah
Now you're talking I can hear you
Go ahead and write
a poem They're wonderful
in bed too kiddo

ECONOMIC CRISES
(Montreal Star, May 31, 1955)

On page 31 a professor says
our economy can't employ all the people we have;

on page 13 a professor says we need more people
to consume all the goods we have.

It's clear we need a population of the "artist type"
who will be willing to consume

without producing
anything Canadians want.

THE RACE

Pine trees that grow 200 feet in the air
and have no green but a bunched Christmas tree
          at the top

have done it through competition
with other trees,
like the armaments race,
          or skyscraper cities,

each trying to get the light from the other,
until all are too far from the earth
to get enough juice,
and suck it a half-mile up
          for a mere living.

ATOMIC RACE

Keep slim or fat, descend or soar,
        You follow nature's plan:
The sequoia has outlived the dinosaur
        The maple will outlive man.

METEMPARADOGPSYCHOSIS

A lady who had fed too many pigeons
thought she'd turn into a dove
when she died,
but the Great Dog made her over into a she-cat
who particularly loved
to kill pigeons.

A CORNET FOR CRITICS

The beauty of being a critic
is that one can write as if one were infallible
and be forever wrong

For if one makes a howling error
of judgment such as casting talent
aside, or throwing obloquy
on genius, or praising an ass

one can forget, later, like one's readers

and praise what one called a bore
as infallibly as before.

NOTE FOR CRITICS

Why do we need mediocrities
To explain great men?

Isn't their greatness in this—
How well they explain themselves?

THE SCHOLARS

All the intensity of art,
its intricate passion and life-paid truth,
but feeds the pomposity of scholars.

Common humanity ignores
what was given; carrion-eaters
fatten on God's meat.

THE PROGRESS OF SATIRE

Reading a dead poet
Who complained in his time
Against bad laws, bad manners,
And bad weather in bad rhyme,

I thought how glad he'd be
To be living in our time
To damn worse laws, worse manners,
And worse weather, in worse rhyme.

CONFUCIAN COMPLAINT

Coffee smells in corridors are acceptable
and even steaks may be pleasant,
but I do not like the smell of undigested oysters
thrown up by an improper tenant
at my doorstep.

EACH AFTER HIS NATURE

Loving a girl whose father and mother object,
should I possess her?

Kung said: Yes, you should possess her.

But the consequences!

In that event, you should not possess her.

DON'T TALK

Lovers have no need to talk

After the act he said
thank you
and thus offended

He should have boasted rather
of his gift
          or said nothing

If you did this for sixteen hours
the perfect lover said
I would let you sleep for eight

So don't talk

A WORD FOR THE LIVING

Certainly nothing we can say
can remove the necessity
of decrepitude and decay;
but having said all that, everything
is still to see and say.
Embryos are not in favour of dying.
Sciatica doesn't attack young dogs.

WELCOME CRITIC

His test,
"the best".

He shows
what grows.

Loves all seeds,
but hates weeds.

IN DAYS TO COME

Every little girl will know a wasp
can cause a swelling,
and every little boy may dream a room
of plush and apples.

All in a bucket will lie
                    the miscellaneous oysters.

But gulls couple-cooing
two by two,
be inseparable, true.

NEW WORLD

How quietly the airship descends
over the roofs of the paltry city—
cleaned up by efficiency experts,
improved by competition,
to this sanity and sanitary urbanity.

I exhort you, citizens,
make your prosperity harder to understand!

THIS CHANGING WORLD

When the last Pope is dead, and the Vatican crypts are open,
there will be—

after
2000 years
of
obfuscation,
inquisition,
forging of documents,
burning,
miseducation,
threats,
persecution
and
prohibition—

A Girl for every boy, and a Boy for every girl
(guaranteed by the state).

EDUCATION

We have our troubles,
a world of 1,500,000,000 illiterates
fed with new ideologies of violence

A few wealthy spots, 6 per cent,
eating up a third of the produce,
and just as ignorant

(e.g. Quebec
where sexless nuns take care of orphans,
turning out schizophrenics)

And "THE CHURCH SEEKS SOLUTION
TO POPULATION EXPLOSION"—
("We recommend legitimate regulation"
—continence, self-control)

O it could be told!

America. . .
Europe. . .
Africa and Asia. . .
(The annual increase "about 30 million"
to feed . . . to educate)

We become animals, ready for slaughter.
Our world philosophies do not suffice.

O MONTREAL

Montreal!
The only city in the world where the sun sets in the North!
City entirely surrounded by sewers,
    one of which provides the drinking water
Ruled by its ten per cent of English . . .
Where money talks— a refined language
And French bombs explode . . .

Greatest frozen inland port
Second largest English-speaking French city in the world
Famous for parking lots . . .

Where the air-pollution in Westmount is not excessive
Where unemployment follows overtime
and layoff precedes holiday . . .

Where newspaper literacy is high
Where poetry doesn't sell

City of bop churches and modern bars
Home of the Montrealer magazine
Emporium of Pinky Stamps and the give-away trade
Teenage harem of NDG (in summer shorts)
Boy nursery (in rags) of St. Henri
Old People's home of Westmount (in tweeds)

You've got marble piles (people kneel in your banks)
You've got the Hydra
You've got leaking gas

You've been sold down the Seaway
You've been had, Montreal! They've shot up your City Center
    —the American way!

Montreal, where's Stanley street?
Montreal, where's my house?
Montreal, where's the red light district I used to know?
Where are your great traditions? where are your historical sites?

Your plaques are rusting!
You don't even know where to dig for Hochelaga!
You've left the Indians in the slum of Caughnawaga
        while you go walking in furs!
You're all blown up inside!

Goodbye! Screw you, Miss Montreal!
Mange les patates frites! Go chez Eaton!

I'm moving to Ste-Agathe where I don't have to look at you anymore
        all through the summer
                (in Montreal, summer is three weeks in July).

REALITY

Once there was so much vision
that even the effort to see things as they are
produced magnificent illusion.
Now, all our effort, no matter how inspired
serves only to show us things as they are.

A LOST ART

The trouble with theatre is
that the most dramatic moments of life
are wordless.

The novel, on the other hand,
has more words than anyone can say
in a mere lifetime.

The true proportion exists
in the poem of course.

THE ROAD DOWN

Art is only a help,
but most people need more help than that.

THE CAGE

Conditioned to the cage, my bird,
whose door is always open
has the whole house to himself
but sits always on his small trapeze, within,
or on top, on wires,
and must be chased off with a stick, forced
to take freedom,
protesting with his loud cantankerous cries,
then back, as soon as danger is over,
to his wire cage, a slave
of first comforts, the fictions defining life
and its limits, stricter than truth.

ONE WORLD

Not only are the asylums overcrowded
but ordinary life is becoming uncomfortable
what with the number of madmen running about.

Nor in our own minds is everything as it should be:
unreasoned fears, rages, faces made in the mirror,
not to speak of cramps and boils, to warn us of it.

And if the political gunmen aren't mad, who is?
There is some discord in nature, I tell you, the atom's split
has ripped the universe, down to the bit fingernail.

EARLY SPRING EMOTIONS

A teenager sitting on the bars
near the High School, her legs spread,
a thin slip of pants
                    covering her crotch,
smiles at me—
            as innocent as they come.

The sun blazes away at the cracked cotyledons
of last year's ragweed, poppy sticks of dead daisies.

Trucks screech
at the bridge intersection, and
a fierce wind blows across the pavement
into dry grass.

I walk delightedly, but chilled,
                        mixing these,
with an angry grimace at the late violence
                    of the cold flashing sun.

LIBERAL CONVENTION

Shrunk in their masks, the Canadian statesmen
grimace before a heart-withered populace.
Technicians surround their lecterns,
wives yawn into the *Globe and Mail.*

And commentators sit like efficiency experts
looking through glass at the sad Sardou comedy
of foible and fret, of blandishment, concealment

the necessary compromise, faking
whatever there is, perhaps, of good
in some, in any of us, in all;

then the masks fall, as in a dream, to show
the naked eyes
and faces, pale and small, sifting election lies.

THE THISTLE

Revelling in the multitude of forms,
verbal and herbal, that life makes and scorns,
I came upon a thistle
convolute, spiked and lean,
in a green field, among buttercups
chickweed and vetch,
a spiked thing, twisted, prickly and mean
(the evil, of which all things have a share,
somewhat concentrated there);
but being so tall I had no fear of him,
I touched his sharp poisoned points
affectionately, bending the vicious stem.

9:

EN MEXICO

EN MÉXICO

I

In waves of weariness,
allergy to foods,
climatic migraine—
such poetry as there was:
of the rudiments of living
in their tropical stir,
storms, and the building trade.

A roar of sea, in constant surrender
to sun and rain,
and palm trees opening genital limbs.

By shores where Cortés landed.

In a world of strangeness
all thoughts run together,
then come singly
like those bell-birds of Vera Cruz.

Beside the ditch the boy was defecating,
as the train passed by he covered his face with his hands.

They live in hovels,
on the harsh crude maguey
that yields string and needle,
paper and twine,
and the hot drink tequila:
beside them the sad dark Mexican,
or a small brown boy with a donkey,
and a woman shielding her mouth with black.

Eat the cactus, own many dogs.

Do the arts matter?
Only as tourist faddle,
                    as the rich man's pride.
From a beginning of adobe huts
and jungle kraals . . .

We have been in the place where hurricanes begin
with hot sidereal spin
taking their rise from the turbulence of the water.

And the dusty horizon
is a dream of distance,
of silence,
then a sudden roar—
among the ruins of blood-hungry gods.

The Cortésian enterprise
turned a continent into a tornado
that rose from this silver spout:
now the jewelry of the cheap stores!

Cortés died old and poor
who was the young Alexander.

As language, it is to be read as language—
the Virgin of Guadalupe,
                    and a brown Mexican mother
leaving the church with her child.
They say 'we all suffer
and therefore pray'.
They say 'we suffer
and Christ, through love,
can release from suffering'—
through love, formed of the love of the mother,
not out of males and females
                                        in their joy.

Guadalupe
        on the road to Teotihuacan.

Here where they killed for the god
            with knives of obsidian,
and the Spaniards "massacred ten thousand"
and the Spaniards "massacred four thousand"
              building crosses.

Yet for us it's only a process
                that a pill can control . . .

We are near to the earth-shaping waves
and the gargoyles of gods,
by the empty palace of Hoon
on the beach at Mocambo.

2

It is most quiet
where it is most violent.
That's why we appear so good.

In a tropical cemetery
hardly a grave is to be seen,
so much is overgrown.

And where Cortés with his men
        (their pockets full of booty)
waded in blood, they've drained the lake
and streetcars glide
where he shook the Indian by the arm and cried:
"You have destroyed the most beautiful city in the world—
                    Tenochtitlan!"

He opened the continent
              like a cornucopia.

Now the jungle has an oceanic luxury:
boys by a heap of papaya
(above them, the cornfields,
                    maguey rows, cactus)
and thatched native huts
with little children in the puddles.
Rain, out of a solitary cloud,
then sun, more sun—
building pyramids of green
and *las flores*
in the Huastecan jungle,
the pre-Aztec world.

On dry-weather roads,
we were speaking of—what?
                The birth of galaxies,
the reproduction of moon-struck snails.
Imagination
          under the beta rays!

How to discover the elements
and to define the natural
and then the skill-won form;
how to reconcile these
with the real conditions
of living, which are universal carnage
in a jungle of fertility—
under the aspect of new knowledge
not of old mythology.

Given the conditions,
energy is there,
     water and sun
     making the jungle.

Then walled haciendas
with all the animals under one roof.

And the temple
of Quetzalcoatl.

Cortés and Moctezuma
two primitive faiths
pitted against each other,
weaving the continental horn.

So Mejicano, mestizo,
have got religion up to the gills,
conferred on them by the Spaniards
(to give enslavement a proper face).

As language. . . Silence is also a language.
When there is no order in heaven
we make what we make
by luck, or strength,
or the composition of desire.
Power grows
like vegetation,
and there are no preferences under heaven.

I do not know why a leaf should be of less worth
than a Vatican,
or why builders care.
The mathematical stones recite their logic
of cruelty and despair—
we arose to gratify some searchless reason
shaping the empty air.

But men have stood on a great eminence
over nature's smoke
when the idea ignited the desire
and desire spoke.

(Even if the idea was wrong, as Teotihuacan
was made to be perfectly functional
as a sacrificial altar.)

How the temple came out of the heart of cruelty,
and out of the jungle the singing birds!

3

Religion,
always used
to put a safe stamp on terror.
First the enemy one hates
is "sacrificed"
then one's own kind—
to contain fear, out of ignorance.
In our time weakness, insecurity, mental pain.

They say no more, as language
(art, or faith)
than any other language;
speak as leaves do,
as dogs sniffing,
as the mating glow-worm sending a call.

And may be wrong.
We make advances
toward "humility".

Religion is an open question.

I thought, seeing the layered stones—
how wonderful
the pursuit of knowledge!
When on the lettered rock-face
appeared a skull and bones.

Optimism is foolish. Life can only be
tragic, no matter what its success.

But the universe does not wait
for me to judge it, nor is death itself
a cause for condemnation.

Knowledge is neither necessary nor possible
to justify the turning
of that huge design.

That turns in the mind, for love.

That it should come into being out of nothing
                                        (grass . . . bird . . . machine and metal),
that they should come into being.
Man come to shape out of smoking matter,
          out of male secretion in the womb, take form.
All things, all bodies,
          that they should come out of nothing,
rise, as projectiles out of rock,
with spicules, eyes, limbs,
with ornaments, accoutrements, skills,
amid an abundance of flora and fauna,
and each to itself all—
in a jungle, devouring graves!

We have passed through the earth's middle
and emerged as we are.
Climbing mountains, living in valleys,
can we miss the end of living?
(Since we have looked death in the face.)
To be is the palm of creation,
and all that we are is seed from a pod.

You may hate the jungle,
its inimical insects, flies,
and the chaos of growing
everything at once;
but we return for fertility
to its moist limbs and vaginal leaves.

They grow over each other, overgrow,
and the whole thing, by elimination,

is also an order that exists.
Hence the necessary magnificence of all reality.
(Where an artist is only a pipsqueak
in a forest of mocking birds.)

So praise the glory of the green jungle
with all its terrible thunders;
praise death and generation
and the embracement of lovers under all skies.
Praise frost and thaw, and the congealing of elements,
or their prismatic flow; praise the disposition of ferns,
and the erection of great trees.
Praise hovels and giant domes
and the ant's most secular mound.
Between cathedral spires
and the plum tree's pleasantness
there is no distinction. Praise these.

Anything we shape in fire,
as anything that grows, by living . . .
There are degrees of beauty.
But as to what makes one flower
more to be prized than another—
we can define the elements, their order,
and what they do in the eye, or mind,
but the shaping hands are undivined.

There is the stubborn, obedient donkey.
And equanimity, as the cow had it
when the busy bus went by.
And thatched cottages, roofs on four sticks,
under which they live
in the mango groves.

(Not to imagine
that we understand anything.
The universe turns
                    me, not I it.)

Imagination makes
the organ cactus,
the autocar,
and a poem with six feet in every line.

And there is intelligence
of the kind that can choose
and of the kind that cannot choose:
the short range of the individual
and the long range of the species
(evolving by generation
                in the moment when we breed,
or answering the immediate need)—
on different time-clocks, yet the same,
a groping fallible mind.

All the green blanketing the hills,
the braided streams,
and the brown sands bleaching;
horses with heads akimbo,
small lambs that leap,
children with huge eyes,
and lovers shy in their look:
            praise these to the bewildering heavens,
knowing no other tongue but praise.

And death also is in the process.
Our bus killed a calf on the road as we passed.
It looked at us coming
then turned into our path as we swerved.
Just a thud, and we kept on going.
(Earlier, we nearly killed a mother and child.)
Not an uneventful voyage.
Those who survive
will have enjoyed the ride.

Perhaps we die
in order to make room for others.
Why should one gang
hold the charabanc of existence for ever?

But what doesn't exist is no matter.
Out of all that death, the real emerges.

Under the shading palms, in the evening hour,
like all creatures who have come to no grief,
like all shoots who have come to flower,
we enjoy the languid air.
There is no travail here,
no passion, pang, or impulse of despair.
The breeze cools the temples with a summer's swell,
and under the tropic starlight all is well.

4

Poetry is my language.

Well nourished, the handsome young
with gentle features, sensitive eyes,
walk the beaches.

Beautiful people,
Creole, Mexican, Spanish
in their variety.
To native music as we heard it at night by the water,
a trio against the tireless surf
singing (forgetting lines)
                                        with plangent voices,
the guitar thwacking and thrumming into the surf beat.

And beautiful servant girls
out of Gauguin, holding their breasts as if for an offering,
bending quiet religious eyes.
One delicate child
of fourteen, in a pink dress,
strolling by with her parents,
so frail and lovely
the air seemed liquid, buoyant about her.

And of larger proportions, grander,
a magnanimous mother with children
dancing toward the shore, in a night-dress,
her opulent ankles tapering
down to her toes
(behind her the children shrieking),
stood poised, supremely graceful,
gigantic—
America, the Continent, dancing.

(What it says is what I ask
of any language. Just because it's 'poetry'
do I have to love what it says?

And you need not hammer
the invincible stones.
Aztec or plastic,
the point of living is the same.)

Here where the sea washes
the uneven shore
(down with the slush, up with the blue water)
the white success is one unbroken line from here to Caleta.
Rolled in a long green hollow,
the sea moss thrashes in the brine, and sand bubbles
or glistens with calcareous triumph
(*now*! *now*! *now*!)
and the men bring sea-shells to their wives,
and young girls flash their stiff buttocks
as the sun strikes the winning nipple—
now! say the strings in singing consummation
we have touched the life-giving current,
making a relay!
Take it from us, you swarming futures!
Sing, as we now sing!

There were women washing
by the edge of a stream, white
laundry on the hedge,

the hard cobbles and knuckles red.
I have looked through glass at the dividing process
and at the war of germs:
after the passion and the split of creation
(foreshadowing death),
look at women by a crystal stream.

Mexico, strange suffering land:
lazy, inflammable,
lacking the meanest comforts.

Dragging their degradations like any people
who have suffered from much rapacity
through generations;
in rotting straw, eating offal,
and serving now the power of cold machines.

Americans everywhere enjoying
the benefits of their poverty and cheap labour.

(Till the guiltiness of an action
is itself the motive for it,
so far have our pleasures been bred to our guilts.)

But we learn the rudiments here,
coming only for play,
removed ourselves from oppression,
by rest, from the common fray.

And that point of perspective shows us
the natural way of survival, and poetry's natural way,
in the stumbling speech of children,
the relaxation of the palm,
the look on a tired woman,
the grin of the happy man.

Where all roads come together
to a place of storm, or sun,
the poem begins proclaiming—"*I-am-that-I-am.*"

5

So Mexico like the poor is happy
with little more to give
than what the tourist takes in glass and beads,
as they took from Cortés in primitive belief.

But the world is changing fast, and faster
than any tourist knows;
                    beliefs, like glass
were never made to last.
We dream, to make them pass into the past.

For out of the jungle, with gigantic roots,
the terror of new knowledge comes, a massive hulk
without bole, without leaves, without fruits. . .
"Great tree! send out your first green shoots!"

The rudiments of living
                        is what we learn:
how rich the undergrowth
before the noble form.

Under the swaying palms, in the heat of the sun,
in the cool of the evening,
for those that have it, or have earned it.

I would not pretend to explain,
learn a stoic silence,
a little joy.

To give with a ready hand to the needy,
and bow before those that die;
                            to accept pleasure.

Since peace should be our reward
                    (only the sea cannot keep still)
when evening comes
and the killing season ends
and animals repose.

The wonder is how we have become used to our world,
the shape of trees, of seeds, of vegetables and fruits,
and have built our own haven of mortar and metal,
in itself as strange—
to become used to that too
as if it were not new
but like the sun and moon in heaven.

We might lick walls,
                    fly, walk on hands,
have wings and tails. . .

The longer one lives
the more tolerance one learns.

To be kind and love
green frogs, ghost crabs, snakes,
all those gentle mechanical creatures
that we kill.
To save man from his insanities.

(With tender affection
I flick an ant to the ground:
"Go along, now.")

After the harsh hills
the great plain opens out before us.
Remember, where we move now
the roads were once cut through mountains.
Beyond, there are more hills.

In the country of the pepper-loving people,
                hot as they say,
who made Maya temples and the marachis—
                                    each in its day.

(Whatever we make, out of the rubble of earth,
not knowing how or why, is like this—
                                    a firelight display.)

When happy, a pleasant people,
never heard to resent each other
                    in the street trade.

Men with wide hats, loose pants,
torn feet, torn hands,
          blasting rock in the sun.
"Dignidad de la persona," declares the news.
So many with open hands.

That students demonstrate
against "aesthetic interests
that have no utility"—
          ni practica ni cultural.

(But to protest against society,
     the universe being what it is?)

Evil is in the warp and weft of reality,
but the whole cloth is good, is good.

The dismal mess notwithstanding.
Wait until the tide comes high.

6

Stars I have never seen before, in the southern sky,
and clouds the colour of roses, of brown trees,
and the *copa de oro* when sun sets
                    in the far sky. . .
I've gazed at the Great Way,
          there is no end to creation.
Cost what it may,
the petals of the infinite flower
     and time loves their sweet bouquet.

Study the way of breaking waves
for the shape of ferns,
               fire and wind
for whatever blows or burns.

Someday we shall come again to the poem
as mysterious as these trees,
                    of various texture,
leaves, bark, fruit
(the razor teeth so neatly arranged,
so clean the weathered root).
There is the art of formal repetition
and the art of singular form—lines clean
                    as a wave-worn stone.

Lizards chucking under the eaves.
Vultures among the leaves.
The comical pelican. The plunging fish.
The coconut used as a dish.

Study the ancient habits
of the most disorderly people.
Where did reason arise?
The science of cleanness—
fastidiousness in art?
Somewhere in this, the market, the church,
                    the commissary.
No matter how steamy the jungle,
small leaves are perfect in detail.
Order remains unimpaired
in man and in matter,
despite all poverty, insanity, and war—
                              the jungle, in its excesses.

From wherever you are, begin!

To the peak of Popocatepetl
seen in the liquid sky
                    (as we came from Taxco)
cutting the air with white precision.

So like the virile leaping of goats
                    in a green valley,
love's restorative power
                              leaps to the heart.

Form is the visible part of being.
We know the logic of its adaptations,
a signature of individuality, of integrity,
the end of perfect resolution—
but not the inner stir.

Rest. Rest in that great affair.

Therefore art is everything;
but not as we imagined.
Art is the way of life.

So the final lines came breaking in due order
in the dust of the wheels;
the green hills falling by,
                                        the words dropped still.

History is always beginning.
Begins from the place we're in.
Creating a past from the future,
collecting "what has been."

I go out
            on a whirling wind,
an explorer's cry in my ears.

Time, time,
            over the clouds,
stretches ahead.

The cumulus grows. The ocean heaves.

Below me, the patterned fields
            lie green, and brown, and red.
Desert and jungle around the fertile plain.

Mexico, there, lies simple and bare—
strange as life anywhere.

P

AT LAC EN COEUR

I

What kind of honey does a bee get from a thistle?
A purple bomb, toxic
        with spears of language.

Hating pretentiousness,
        or the vanity of writing poems,
I sit for hours without a word.

The hidden bios, cosmos, works with his emotions
shaping things into multiform shapes of desire.

He never says a word
        nor even (perhaps) thinks a thought
but fits the liver under the beating heart
as the artist places his cove and tree,
        feeling his way
        to the complex unities.

We cross-section this work of love
        when we think or talk.

2

Nothing is eternal. Not even the trees
though I gather that some are longer-lived than a man.

A whirling flashlight
        makes a permanent wheel.
Moving lights. We are a web.

Unity, out of motion and diversity,
        as real as atoms.

The blue sky turning pale green at the horizon,
only one streak of cloud
        beyond the birch leaves overhead.

The trees, cedar, some maple, and tattered pine,
below them the fern and smaller brush,

dead leaves, brown earth, rock
(a canoe on the still water makes a slapping sound)

And I sit, the ache in my bones receding,
          a thought breathing cold air—

shaping a world already made
          to a form that I require.

3

Since all things contemplate themselves
a mouse in a ditch
          observes itself,

in silence, slips underground
in solitude eats, twitches, curls and sleeps. . .

Does no one approve? No one care?
How can he exist—
          alone?

A mouse goes without fear, alone, as if
          with love's eye upon it.

4

Cottages like Chinese lanterns
          shine in the soft dark
I breathe the moist night, by the lakeside

Fishes peer at our intrepid lights,
          ephemeral man-blown stars
in their familiar trees

The road is lit by a small lamp
waving with my body's swing,
          rocked at the pelvis, to and fro,

as I pass, leaving the great
shadows behind
and the green domes in the night.

5

Some men murder fishes, others kill quail
all for sport. The trees fall
like great sick animals, eaten by the saprophytes in their sides.

We have no time, to hate or mourn.
Love the arrowy fern, mean moss, and furry bee
enough to forgive all

fools out of despair
that, dying, cover fear
with laughter, guns, or game on a hook.

6

Alone in the forest
I hear the wind overhead,
see the lake through the trees.

Several monsters are allayed.
I sit on a high rock, alone,
listening to the wind, looking through the pines.

In front of me a fir
sends up a central stalk
with four pedicles around it

(only by keeping apart from the others
can it assert that form)

curving from the four corners, a cup, kylix
(a word, language),
below this the various branches

end in four-pronged stems,
one, the longest, bearing the end-bud,
others minors, keeping proportion.

The whole thing somewhat isolated
                from the smothering multitude—
a complete architecture of organic meaning.

Perfect to live, alone, lonely,
aspiring and self-fulfilled, growing, in a cleft,
                on this high rock,
with only the wind and sky to see and hear.

7

But a flower torn off from the stem does not know
what a tragedy has occurred,
                        a waterlily

opens and closes with the day
                        on our table
as though it were a vase in a lake.

Rootless flowers!
whose individuation is yet a part of their form. . .

To live, become immune
            to every bleeding cosmic wound.

8

The shapes, I think them
                as of waves coming in
                lapping the curve of the shore,
                                and wind carving clouds,
may be or not be as I perceive

but the fruit of the maple, pine cone,
seed of the cedar (proving Goethe's principle,
            every compartment
a form like the flattened branch and whole tree)

formed out of the flux, are there
atomic, mobile—
        unities that persist,
real as in a mind.

9

Who thinks the living universe?
I think it but in part.
Fragments exist
                    like those infinitesimal separate stars
I saw, lying on my back on the cushions
last night before the storm:

their union, as powers
                  but as wheels on the one axle,
and as form—
           a drawing by a master hand.

We have united some few pigments
                (all that is in museums)
but the greater part, all life, was there
                                        united when we came—
and grows, a copious language of forms.

Who thinks them? . . .
                  Their being is a thought.

My thought, a part of being—is a tree
of many thoughts, in which a yellow bird sits.

10

In the silence, sitting in the silence
I seem to hear the visible language speak
                                                    a leaf
(a glimpse of paradise perhaps to be)

Here in hell, in purgatorio,
all things suffer this waiting, become
only then whatever they will be:

ecstasies of creation, flowers
          opening ecstatic lucent leaves.

Nothing else matters.
Nothing else speaks.

II

So beauty
it says, so quietly in the shadows
that a small bird
          on a red bomb
shrieks a symphonic whistle
just turning its head, without a sound from the throat.

Anywhere the eyebeam transects the world, a thorn
strikes with such sharpness to a thought.

LAC EN COEUR

I had so far made it my concern
          not to be aware
of writing a poem, thought of it
as irrelevant,
as in this case anyhow contrary
          to my real concern,

that I wrote nothing
          I did not first think
complete, as it stands.
Not a poem, but a meditation—
          they make themselves, are also natural forms,

kernels that come whole to the hand.

10: SELECTIONS FROM ATLANTIS

PROLOGUE

Of voyages: there was Ulysses' voyage,
and Cortés, the great adventurers.

But even suburban dwellers
voyage, though they commute, eat toast, get their magazines
on time
even a beggar in front of Morgan's
voyages on his worn-out magic carpet of cold.

The voyage is still the prototype—
touristic now, because we city people
do not slosh through blood
but live in glass observation cars of boredom.

One could not write a poem waiting for the train to start.
But once in motion, well in motion
how is it possible not to begin?

Travel is the life-voyage in little,
a poem, a fiction, a structure of illusion!
And then you ask, 'What does it mean?'

Voices, baggage, a girl's knee,
and bells, distant, obscure
Every object a word, language, the record we make
a literal transcription,
then a translation
into moral, abstract meaning.

Travel, to and from (the place does not matter)
the Ding an sich in a mirror—
Let it speak!

Anyone who travels
sees others at the crossroads.
There is more than one road.

Who knows where the others may lead to?

There are infinite worlds: green lights,
highway lines, homes,
power stations and industrial domes.

All these things are other people's lives,
effective symbols of their discovered desires.

And what new road lies ahead? What
out of our living centre may we not create?

(I can be as cynical as the rest of them.
It is more difficult to reconstruct these illusions
than to destroy them.)

But to write poetry in a crowd of people?
The self is drowned. A 'lost illusion'.
When illusion itself is blurred—
are we nearer to reality?

Chaos!
A bad knee, or neuralgia,
less real when everything is clear
than chaos which is alive, like that dime
that rolled along the floor—
"A living thing."

Too many illusions
blur Pietro, Carbuio, Stefano and me into a oneness.
A chaos of Italian
prepares a renaissance,
at least of wonder!

How seagulls know what they are!

So to be, whatever you are—
a white bird,

a man with a blue guitar.
But there is room for more, more.

It is the part of us
not yet finished as seagull or man
that worries us at the pit of creation,

hanging over cliffs, drowning,
or lifted in flight

to new states of being, asking always what we are.

Like this ship leaving, gently, to silent tears
falling all around,
the infinite poem begins, with its power
of a great ocean-liner greeting the waves,
bound for the sea, its home.

So the waves of the sea (it all comes back to me
as when I first heard it),
the white snowcaps breaking,
the power of repetition, multitudes,
like the universe of atoms—

ephemeral, too, the making and breaking
of crested forms.

It comes back to me
(like a wave in these waters)
in the repetition of these lines.

I will tell you what it is with the society of ship-folk.

They make the effort to mix, out of baser elements,
the cheap coin of their private lives,
a new reality, but cannot

(forget those who want a good time,
are young and pretty and find it).

It is here that the dentist, the lawyer, the housewife,
the teacher,
try to meet for the first time
hoping to be made into something new.
"A man should be free"
"I never interfere with my sons, never!"
"You should forget about money . . ."

Are bored (the lawyer is bored with the dentist,
the dentist is bored with the teacher):
their structured selves stick out,
as lawyer, doctor, housewife, clerk

(forget the young, who have no past to shatter,
who want a good time
and take it in any form).

The middle-aged want a new life, but do not find it,
not on this voyage.
Perhaps they think that death will be a new reminting.

One never knows about people.
The gay ones we started with
have come up with secret illnesses, private griefs;
lovely girls proved dull, selfish, or vain,
the scholarship winner a tongue-tied boy.

But the middle-aged one might have ignored
one cannot now forget.

The dark lady who told me she was never entirely at home,
in Italy or in America,

and the Albanian whose language we explored—
Perendy for God,
shurf for death.

There are some whose talk is salty and seasoned,
who do not care at all for what you say.

They've found their way, and will not be changed
for pleasure or loud mercurial chatter.

These corals are excellent samples,
            the end, perhaps, of long searching and care.

(Lukewarm Canadians! As if anything but the extremes
            of any ideal were worth a damn . . .

What you want is not 'compromise'
            but a powerful combination of virtues!)

Speaking of coral, the white whirling wave
behind the ship
is like a Japanese painting of a wave.

It is not the painting that is like a wave
but the wave like a real painting—
as exact, as detailed, as white and delicate,
made of many tiny hands, of drops, of lacing lines,
a continuous flocculation of white light
that is unlike mere water as a Rembrandt is unlike mere paint.

That nature is the prime artist does not mean that
            all nature is art.
The means are wasteful, but the occasional fragment
may be a masterpiece, a poem, or even a man.

Chatter is like churning water,
            a formless deformation of words.

Real speech, eloquence,
            demands an occasion—
a ritual (today is Palm Sunday).

It seems so easy
but about a page or so a day is what it comes to—
            no more. Sometimes better.

The search for meaning's a sudden compacting
of thought that took maybe days or years—
the poem a crystal
        formed in an empty cave of time.

And it would be far more difficult, almost impossible,
to write a poem in the rhythm of another, earlier, poem
than to write a new one, in the rhythm of a new one.

Reading in passage, in mid-ocean, in the midst of Italian
                                        people,
Silone, and Rostovtzeff on Rome,
the real Italians chattering, the real cafoni,
            with *sciocchezza* and *chiacchiera* on either side,
neither cute numskulls nor comic innocents
                as depicted in the tradition
they are of all kinds:
Rostovtzeff tells their earliest history
        (blood flowing through the arches of the Colosseum).

Roman history is a tale of snarls and murderous fangs,
            greed forever impelling the extortionist's hand.
The Gracchi only accelerated the super-state
            crashing toward absolutism.
                            (Can we arrest it?
            Provide a program—of "Order and Freedom"?)

One learns that great evil, like great good,
        is not the property of any people,
                        but is a monopoly of the state—
or a disease of noble minds corrupting desire.
These Italians were already subjugated under Rome;
for them the Gracchi spoke, the slaves revolted and failed.
They are the remnants of the oppressed through time.
Of those who survive, few were masters, most
        are born paupers. They suffered and here they are.

If you want to know what the "Class system" really is
            take a sea voyage.

Same as on land, in cities,
only more legibly defined:
Limit of the Third Class,
sour oranges,
lousy films (first run features are being shown
in the First Class),
poor service, cheap wine.

Same as on land, where money
chalks out the limit of the Third Class—
restaurants you do not go to,
smart hotels,
food you do not buy, entertainments
bad service and wine,
cheap tenements.
An ocean voyage
can be a lesson in politics and economics, as well as love.

I suppose the Russians will make the revolution—
a classless ship!

We're looking for chaos, the laws of freedom,
where there is so much failure, of concretion,
and petrifaction.

I can hardly see the white light or the flow of foam
through the black pigments and structure of matter.

If one could always leave a ship, an old mess,
as easily as this one . . .
But we continue, dragging our failures,
like excrements, behind us.
As if there were not enough fresh substance, uncreated,
to mould into new being.

Though we must build on the past, like the genes,
and nature in us is limited (since nothing
comes of nothing),

everything still can be made of what is there.
The multiplicity of chaos, our actual lives
whatever they are, leaves us
free to take the pieces, in any order, and move
                                        with new desires.

"I hate travel"
but all the poetry I've written seems to be about travel.
Like this voyage . . . (all life's a voyage
        and any small voyage is a lifetime in little).

Leisure and pleasure (whatever that is)
                test even one's capacity for boredom—
the calcified clinkers of other men's minds.

One "passenger" is a former Fascist soldier
                        in the armies of Mussolini,
surrendered in Sicily, taken prisoner

to America, married to a U.S. citizen.

Now, sixteen years later, himself an American,
he is returning to Italy as a visitor.

Italian politics doesn't interest him,
his conversation is very dull.

He is burdened with a drab dumpy wife
                that he exchanged for his army record.

His real identity is buried in the Libyan sands.

Today we passed over Atlantis,
                which is our true home.
We live in exile
waiting for that world to come.

Here nothing is real, only a few
actions, or words,
bits of Atlantis, are real.

I do not love my fellow men
but only citizens of Atlantis,
or those who have a portion
of the elements that make it real.

One day at sea, at sunset,
when the long rays struck the water,
it seemed to me the whole sea was living
under the surface motion;

the waves moved like a great cosmic animal
twisting and turning its muscular body
under the grey glistening skin.

And I thought that land also is such a body,
and all men, and all living things—
the life within made invisible, or hardened,
or covered with deep hard crust,

until it is scraped or dug for, or cleared away,
or with love reached, or by art or other good,
seen for a moment—

like a great cosmic animal, of great power, of great beauty.

Eidolons, visions of that reality
in moments of illumination,
are the things we love.

The last girl I was in bed with
was very gentle and kind.
She knew the bodily peculiarities.
We sat talking quietly for an hour,
then love began.

True lovers are wonderfully generous and kind.

Those who cannot love
prohibit love to others.
But the will to power is fury against the need to love.

These hours are of no interest—
I sit and stare.
Wait for the words to come.

They appear with new perception, a flash of light,
mere words—"A wonderful voyage . . ." "Monkeys!"
(at Gibraltar)—
or you hear "mare nostrum" in the air.

I go to drink coffee, expecting nothing,
hoping that the gods are kind.

Conquest by force is possible,
but real conquest is moral.
If there is no superior life to bring in there is no victory,
or the conqueror himself may be overcome.

Marble is the cross-section of a cloud.
What, then, if the forms we know
are sections of a full body
whose dimensions are timeless
and bodiless, like poems,
whose unseen dimension is mind?

I want to learn how we can take life seriously,
without afflatus, without rhetoric;
to see something like a natural ritual,
maybe an epic mode unrevealed,
in the everyday round of affairs.

The touch of land, solid under sea-legs,
touch of the present
          no matter how sad or poor.
Even in ignorance, to have something we can believe in
                    to stand on.
To join in the crowd.

I was never so moved to imagine
                the alternatives of being
as in the midst of the sea's commotion—
                    the clouds and wave-rolls
out of which these islands are formed
        like porphyritic stones under Vesuvius.

But land is delightful
After an interval of dreaming, of vertigo,
                              of suspension,
to walk again on soil, the sand
on which our cities and ephemeral homes are built.

From PART I

Ah, Napoli!
Vesuvius and Somma in clouds,
the climbing streets,white and light green in the sun,
                lemon trees
(in the afternoon, fireworks for the festa),
children, tumblers of all ages,
and below, the city—a pastel white—and the bay
(any city on a mountain has beauty,
some form of action, relief—but a mountain, and a bay!)
And the Funicolare, to take you up,
and the wines . . . the cheeses . . .
the sellers of flowers, and the walls
            covered with climbing green . . .
Singing voices outside the window, a cockcrow
                    every morning:

I know the world has no other city
like Naples.
For Italy,
it's their Aglaia—
a kind of aesthetic joy, key to their secret life.

The mistake of Montreal was to have made the mountain
a park
which nobody uses—
not even the poets, anymore,
when they might have built as in Naples
beautiful open terraces on a hill.

But even their rich homes are enclosed
pompous preserves of privacy.
They would have ruined it,
even if they had taken the chance.

And there are more beautiful houses here, I think,
than any architect could have devised or dreamed.
The ideas must have come like mushrooms and ferns
in a jungle.
The place is a chaos made of beautiful things.

I ragazzi!
Lighting a firecracker at the bottom of the stairs.
I watched it go off
with a piang!
And the children shrieked.
Then they played for marbles
(the great and the small).

I wonder if we would die of happiness
if we did not suffer.
Are we afraid to try?

There are too many people. Of course there are too
many people.

But they haven't ruined the world.
They only make it more difficult to survive
        (in ten years, or a hundred, we may need more men).
The point is not to stop breathing
                                but to make room for more.

Even the dirt is necessary.
It's some kind of beauty in ruin,
                                like a falling rose.
Even new dirt contributes to beauty,
        it is what we have to do, if we want to live.

But for any people, their life is visible
                in the kind of beauty they create.

Architecture, sculpture—
                correspond to the body-build.
Looking at windows, you can tell
                                        the ideal Italian
                                                would be graceful, lean.

It doesn't matter that most are short and fat.
Like a miss in darts—
        in his children, the thrower still aims.

In a way, it's one vast slum,
                                the world.
Or a rich garbage dump
on which gaudy flowers and delicate pinks
                        sprout, clamber, float;

a ghostly beauty rising over decay

on tip-toe stems, hardly touching the earth,
        points of transparent, watery dew.

Or Mount Vesuvius smoking
—you think it isn't beautiful?
Or terrifying?

Or Italian women
—reality!
beside the Petty girls of art!

When those Hungarians
first came to Montreal
there wasn't a place where you could sit down for a cappucino
No wonder they started to set up restaurants.

You've got to make something out of what is there
and make it true
to that reality like nothing else, like no one else, in you.

It is no wonder the Italians love their country
(palm trees like rocket fireworks,
trees out of Leonardo),

and like to set up monuments,
and make sculptures
adding to abundance.

It is no wonder they gave life to the new Europe,
birth to the modern.

Praise to this people,
praise even to bluff and strut
and loud oratorical flourish.

They feel who they are, in all that poverty and dust,
and will at least re-enact it!

But Diaz, Ethiopia . . . wars

What's the use of talking about wars?

The war that's coming
may help us to forget any war that ever was.

(The Angel of Poetry
              must be different from any other angel
—of sex, or war

When he saw me standing there,
                                        completely unemployed
he decided to come down

And this is somehow his good,
              not mine.)

A poem is like a living animal.
If you look at any poem really close
you will discover its anatomy.

Under the skin are veins, tendons, nerves
that move and hold it together.

When the girl said she hated lizards
                                                  at Pompei
I thought: It's all in the family, you know,
                    we are all lizards.

If you loved all of it, you would also love lizards.
It's only a part of yourself you hate.

Look at your hand!

One way to solve the tourist problem
would be to admit no one without a speaking knowledge
                              of Italian—
like a graduate course in art or language.

What happens to a city
when five million people go through it in a summer?

For one thing, the valves of hospitality may close
—it becomes a business.

Even the walls of the museums must be worn out.

And the people, with their doors in the narrow streets,
with their bimbi, and bags,
what have they to do with Empires,
or art, or a Renaissance of power?

They are the eternal soil,
the raw matter of mankind.

To understand their little corner shrines
remember that it was Jesus
who first taught us to think of the poor and
to love them.

The plaster is still falling
on some of the walls of Pompei

But the lovely lizards
are very much alive!

The past is a lost dimension.

(For relief, I used an old toilet
once employed by the Romans.
What better
than to bring life to old ruins?)

Unless we can see it live, it is a deep unknown—
an Id
that may strangle us in our sleep.

At Pompei, the American gentleman
wanted to know whether the trees had been planted
by the Romans.
"Who planted them?" he asked the guard.

Beautiful letters on the wall.
(Nietzsche walked here,
and Henry James, and before that, Goethe.)

Anch' io. Canadese.

Why do we stand in awe of the past,
as if something that long ago
must have been different, even fearful?
We are afraid of the possible unknown!
The dead may reach out of the darkness and terrify us
with the real possibilities of the present.

For instance the ruins you can see anywhere in Naples
(crumbling houses)
and the ruins of Pompei—
which would we rather not see in ruin?
And which are really best, as ruins?
How terrible if they were still alive!
But you can buy oranges with a few twigs and leaves
for completeness,
and lemons grow over your head as you drink coffee.
How's that for life?

Bella, bella. Sei bella.

Bella ragazza, bella figliuola,
bella signorina!
(*Anche bel garzone.*)
Tutti bellisimi. Tutti!

Come un giardino, come una siepe
coronata dei fiori!

Bacciamoci . . .
i belli ginocchi, labbra, occhi.

E lasciami con un grido d'amore.

The point is, no matter how great or powerful was the past,
there is only the present,
and the past exists only as the present,
it moves us, and it is present
because it moves us.

What we discover of the past is what we use,
nothing else is real.
Time is the illusion
that makes all existence null and void
and cleaves to what is living still.

So Rome is Khrushchev, America.
What was once the state is now a machine.
And the dead artists who painted walls
are cutting flowers on Italian glass.
Nothing is lost, the world is fuller than it ever was.
What is cut down in one quarter
is probably somewhere that much more alive.
And if the whole world should perish,
do you think the powers that made us would fold up and die?

. . .

But I have been in a marine aquarium and I have seen

LOLIGO VULGARIS
TRACHINUS ARANEUS
SCORPAENA SCROFA
SCYLLARIDES
ANEMONIA SULCATA
ASTEROIDES CALYCULARIS
MAJA SQUINADO
MUSTELLUS LAEVIS

THALASSOCHELIS CARETTA
TRIGLA CORAX
TRYGON VIOLACEA
HYPPOCAMPUS BREVIROSTRIS
SPIROGRAPHIS SPALANZANII
ACTINIA CARI
MURAENA HELENA
SYNGNATUS ACUS
RETEPORA MEDITERRANEA
PELAGIA NOCTILUCA
PARAMURICEA CHAMALEON

Of a very graceful undulant movement
of a pale white colour
with translucent fins

Fish that lie buried in the sand, on the sea bottom,
with only their eyes peering out

Or long and thin as a pencil
flexible in movement

Or absurd, barnacled, monstrous bulldogs of the deep,
and sea-spiders of gigantic size.

Red flowers of the sea
(or orange coloured)
like carnations, like broken pieces of pomegranate

(I too was once a fish
I rubbed myself on the sea bottom, leaping gracefully
A large fish, about two feet long)

There was one like a great sturgeon
constantly moving and twisting its muscular body

And a fish with tentacles under the fins
on which it walks on the sea floor!
It has a blue fin, that opens when it swims

And speckled fish, too, with the eyes of snakes
at the bottom of the sea, their heads gently bobbing

And an Octopus
with saucer-like suckers, a paunchy body,
huge eyes on great mounds,
blowing out of intestinal tubes,
coiling the tips of his tentacles like a seashell.

He looked intelligent
Maybe he is intelligent, I thought, like a poet
or a philosopher
who understands, but cannot act to circumvent clever men.

The octopus opened his magnificent umbrella,
pushed the belly forward, and bumped into a sleeping fellow
Then he went behind a pilaster
because I had been watching him too long.

A magnificent creature.

And I saw beautiful tiny sea-horses
with a fin on the back
vibrating like a little wheel
And a ghostly shrimp six inches long
light pink and white
and graceful as a star, or the new moon

And a whorl of delicate white toothpicks
And brown stems, with white strings like Chinese
bean-sprouts, long and graceful.

And I saw a wonderful turtle.

But I have seen fish, turtle, octopus, with dead eyes
looking out at the world.
What is life doing? waiting for something to come?
Are we all stepping-stones to something still unknown?

Is man, when he is glad, when he is in love or enthralled
at last getting a glimpse of it?
Are the birds? Are the swift fish?

(Or perhaps they know they are captive. Who can tell,
even a fish may know when it is not at home.)

Then I saw a thin, thin thing
undistinguishable from a twig (just a few inches long)
but on close inspection very beautiful.

Since he has disguised himself to look so unremarkable,
for whom does he keep that secret form?

There was a light green jelly
PHYSOPHORA HYDROSTATICA
And a kind of huge one-foot-long paramecium
PYROSOMA GIGANTEUM

And a thread-like plant with fragile white hair
(They say the chromosomes are such a thing of diminutive
size, the whole life contained in their genes!)

And a coral that was a true artistic design
made by a growing plant—
a Persian decorative motif.

And many other intelligent plants, animals, and fish.

From PART II

1

The Greeks could see a god and say,
"Why, it's only a man."
But we, who know only men, want to see God.

In the church which is already music (Notre Dame),
wrapped in many coats against the grim cold,
                    we heard the Requiem of Brahms.
The old cathedral seemed to shake
          so that we feared for the glass in the precious windows
when the music of the sopranos and the bass
        combined in solemn chorus
                    with strings, flutes, and brass.
And when the Requiem was ended,
            why did no one applaud?
Because to praise men is foolish who have praised God.
There is something more than man, we all know it,
            that like a Requiem silences human applause.

But then we have the Eichmann trial.

Eichmann is not important
          and those who are now dead no longer suffer.

(Four thousand children shipped from Paris,
taken from their mothers, hungry, hurt, sick,
sleeping on sacks, on floors,
                    in September,
screaming, to the cold freight cars,
                across Germany, Poland,
to Auschwitz.
              They no longer shriek or suffer.)

Those millions, beaten by truncheons,
                        scarred by surgery,
who ran with bleeding feet, do not suffer.

They are dead now. They are gone.

Hitler could not take from them that final good.

They do not suffer.

It is we who must think of them still.

And Beethoven will be forgotten, and Goethe,
and the great mind of Kant (when Germany is gone),
but men will say: *They did this.*

The living are not "responsible"!
It is not a matter of blame!
(No man is to blame for what another did.)

But monumental good and monumental evil
are the twin realities whereby we exist . . .
And great evil outdarkens all good.

We may commit that crime
which will destroy all the good deeds of mankind.
'What others did' marks the way;
is both an invitation and a warning.
It shatters our life—of small fears and aims!

I met a very pleasant German girl, with her parents,
on a visit to Paris for a few days.
We talked over the table. I walked her home.
She expressed herself with difficulty in English.
Who thinks more of Auschwitz, she or I?

Who visits the Louvre?
Or who owns the Parthenon frieze?

The sea belongs to whoever sits by the shore.

Say it again. What happened
is nothing to the millions dead, who suffered;
nor are the living to blame.
(In a hundred years, or two hundred, this will be plainly true.
The action only exists, and is real, apart from the men
who bear it, or have a part in it,
as a measure of what we can still do.

If we end the world, in what would be the greatest crime,
it could only happen because we had already prepared for it
with earlier committed crimes.

("This could never have happened in 5000 B.C.")

All evil begins with the first crime,
and just as the good has grown
so the magnitude of evil grows.
The Massacre of the Innocents began with the murder of Cain
And the palaces of art are filled with tortures and knives
as well as Saints and Madonnas with gentle eyes.

History is an explosion of the human heart.

Put it
that the power to do good is always equal
to the power to do evil,
and we have never stopped doing both.

France is the conscience of Europe.
One considers these things:
Camus,
L'Affaire this-or-that,
or the current news.

Where the best men are political
(not that the political are best)
and even journalists can think.
"Head leather," the French call the scalp.

Of course, Hitler thought he was doing good—
"everything is relative".
And "who are we to judge"?
I put it to you, gentlemen,
draw the conclusions!
(Can you hear Mrs. Grundy's applause?)

But only those who break the laws make the laws.
"The moral law within us"—though we must dig for it
through the crust of Mrs. Grundy's laws.

It's odd how we fear the unknown
more than anything known.
As Rilke said, ". . . it disdains to destroy us."

Several times, I said, "I have lived.
If I die after this I am satisfied."
It is not a shadow.

The secret of translation:
English Spoken
Se Habla Español.
From gods to men.
The world, the language of God.

3

All the infinities, perfections,
ecstasies, all magnificence—
belong to man.

He was to be perfected, praised, desired,
loved forever and glorified!

Let us go out to look for handsome athletes,
happy lovers, poets at café tables
(even statesmen and business managers),
wise teachers we have not seen
who are not in the clouds;
e.g., a brass-plate cleaner oiling his elbows
or singing workmen on a high rigging;
even an efficient traffic cop.
(No men in armour, no equestrian statues.)
A "business lunch" may be a beginning—
with facts and figures

(you, Ron Everson)
The Champs Elysées for Elysian fields,
                    Mount Royal a seat for kings.

Hell is a human place, but so is heaven:
the whole Comedy at our doorstep.

Look, the king of Belgium
        riding past the Grand Palais (shadows of royalty)
                    with De Gaulle.
Hurrah!
Enthusiasm shakes the crowd.

The three eternities: we have within us
                    a paradise of contemplation.
(Do we need proof that hell is possible?)
We need all three.

"Qui sont les plastiqueurs?" asks Sartre.
(Qui sont les justes? les vrais?)
At lunch-time you see women
        lugging a bottle of wine and a loaf of bread.
Between rich people taking their sunbaths
        and the poor eating sandwiches,
there's a purgatory in the middle.

Politically speaking, the uncommitted—
                    the danger zone.
Ask for the king! the possibilities!

Around l'Etoile is the part of Paris I dislike,
        rich slums (though there are always good people).
Let the pseudo-paradise be dissolved!

There is the heaven of Montparnasse.
And the old heaven of Notre Dame.
And a new heaven, broken, waiting to be gathered.

How common in daily use is hell!
We're not supposed to believe in the devil!
As though our hell were here, our heaven there,
                    and all between an emptiness.

Modern man believes in hell, certainly,
but not in any good, nor any possible salvation.

He takes the literal meaning: 'Dante's Inferno'.

But there is waking that is like sleep,
                              a reverie, without argument,
a pure perception.

Allness.
Amo. An open door.

Like a long thought, a sweet remembering, without words.
All-over light everywhere. A gentleness.

There is act, gift, without afterthought.
          (Do it and run, don't look back!)
A real exception.

No ugly face.
Beauty without desire. Love without action.
                         A perfect reward.

I shall creep in.
I shall lie waiting.
I shall look for a chance.

There, they are waiting for us!
Who?
               Everyone!
                                        Oh, hurry!

The butterflies are dancing (lights on the Seine)
spilling a box of feathers.

Bulles Bleues.
Someone forgot his clothes!
O joy!

They are all running together.
Is it love?
Who cares!
Yes!

Look at the lovely banner:
ABANDON
(I can't read)

Abandon something.
It looks like they've abandoned it.

(Don't laugh. It can happen to you.
I hope it will.)

There isn't a soul left in the city.
They're all up there.
What a celebration!

Paradise, is it?

We take our heaven in small doses.
It's safer that way, for all concerned.

"Berkeley in his youth described the *summum bonum*
and the reality of Heaven as physical pleasure . . ."

Time floats like an island
in the sea of being.
We must study
its birds and flowers as language
that tells us our past and future.
For there is no other knowledge.

Think of the idiots who want a "vision",
having the sun-blasted world before their eyes.
It has been given!

We have only to read the signs.
What would it be to me if I heard voices
                    (I hear your voice);
What if I saw a spirit
                              (when I see your face)?
It is impossible not to read the signs.
The very eyesight speaks, and the ear sees,
while all the visionaries grope in the dark.

We do not see;
as greatness does not know itself—
Rousseau and Voltaire facing each other in their tombs,
                                 under the Pantheon.
Voltaire who "would not go on all fours".
Rousseau, who chided wit.

An opaque mountain of books
          stands between man and man.
Yet all the senses read
               in the knobbled braille of things.

My favourite reading place in Paris
                                        was a small park
by Saint-Julien-le-Pauvre
with the old church at the back
                         and the cathedral in front,

the traffic passing by, and children at play
               (new ones asleep in their mothers' arms),
and languid lovers on the shady seats, holding hands.

A beautiful woman on a bench
          with a line of cars behind her.
The hedge, the fence, the trees
                              like a poem on a page.

But actually the trees speak an older meaning:
I look at the wandering trunks, the leaves,
          the dark serenity of silence
that no one in the city sees.

There are people who think of books only as "dirty stuff".
"The kind of thing you get in books."
And of course there's the trade in "the nude":
LE NUS JAPONNAIS etc.
(To cure us of it, everyone should walk naked for a year.)
It's an old metaphor, the world as a used book.
Read it literally—keep God out of it—
or read between the lines.

E.g., the Sainte Chapelle,
—no need to insist on the beauty of fireworks.
You can "see" God.

No one has to affirm life,
we hold on to it desperately enough.

I suppose part of all beauty, like a clean slate
or a new canvas,
is the pleasure of knowing it can be spoiled.
The promise of untried experience.

(There is also the courtesy of the audience.
One should applaud a little
even if the work is not very good.)

As pure art, it is Psyche—
the ballerina's butterfly body.
For what is spirit
if not the potentiality of things?

(Not the supreme good of the Soviets, the state
as the superego.
"Don't look under my skirt," the Iron Curtain,
or self-righteousness that cruelly castigates the child.)

Inono no vaovao ("What's new?")
Raphia, Aleurite, Sisal,
Ylang-ylang, vanilla, lemon grass.

"Inevitable communism" says my friend.

A problem for psychoanalysis, all politics
        is a problem for psychoanalysis.
In crisis, an incipient psychosis.

We read the wrong meaning. Mostly
                                a misuse of mind.
Piss has corroded the sidewalks of Paris.
What sort of poetry is that?

DANS CETTE MAISON HABITA
What is it?
        Cabaret   Music-Hall   Dancing
                                JOCKEY
                            "ON S'Y AMUSE"
A tragi-comedy, mock-romantic realism.
L'absurde.
        Or comic surrealism . . .
An infinite défilé of the finite.
A puzzle with private answers.
An opportunity.

In the Cimetière Montparnasse
                Sainte-Beuve
                Laurens
                АЛЕХИН
                Coppée
        LA COMMEDIA È FINITA

Some of the names illegible
Or so new, they died "en déportation"
                            in Germany, or Poland
"Love one another."
"Les morts sont invisibles, ils ne sont pas absents."

Yet we either want to learn it from great men
or have it handed to us
                by "an ordered society".

It is really each man's business—
with taste, toast, monkey, or mistress.
"Let's see what you can do now."

There's some bit of satisfaction
that eternity must extract
even from every human failure.

The statistical chaos is a soup-pot of succulent cooking.

Imagine a subway-stop called
MONTPARNASSE-BIENVENUE
And almost in every train there are lovers standing
practically doing the works in public.
"Je n'entends pas par là ce que vous appelez en France l'amour,"
said Arthur Miller to the interviewer
(probably travels by taxi),
while in America "sex is the only thing real".

There is no doubt that Soviet Russia represents for the world today
what America did in the last century
("Air from the Caucasus" in their Métro).

Here a man lies curled up on the griddle
with a bottle beside him:
PRIMIOR Notre Vin Quotidien.

CRICKET: name for a cigarette lighter.
NECTAR: a pure-bred pony
whose father was Rantzau and mother Frieda
(a thing of beauty)
And we try to sew together the human body
and whatever else it is made of,
but cannot do it.

Mem. A permanent address book for great men.
Voltaire, Marie-Arouet. Panthéon No. 1.

There's a kind of ideal beauty
O so frail and powder-pale

The food of poets
Miss millefeuille, not a promise of experience
but of pure heaven
(in the shuttle, between sex and love).

For the Greeks, it wasn't man's body that was beautiful
but the god in man that was beautiful.

Most of what we see is absurd.

Now the novelty is gone. And now that the place is familiar
and real, it can tell us nothing.
Only the unfamiliar and unreal
continually become, or promise to become—real.

The fact that one is leaving
makes it even more unreal.
Adieu, ma belle.

Happy the man who has some world he loves,
that he can call his own,
to which he can return.

Like the waitress in the café
hugging her mug of café-au-lait,
to whom the streets belong, the street markets, the shops,
the men,
and life is a round of genial affairs.

Without it there is no *beau voyage*,
only homelessness,
a world of strangeness that is not a place.

Adieu Paris.

"Ta bouche est comme un sandwich très délicieux.

"Je cherche tes puces.
"Il n'y a rien, rien. C'est le néant.
"Il faut changer notre vie."
"Mais les Américains ont acheté le monde, hélas,
"avec le drapeau rouge à cinquante-quatre plis."

"On a trouvé hier soir
"un poète noyé dans une bouteille de Coke."

Where are the gods, in the dreaming stone
The Cnidian Aphrodite
                    of transfigured desire

The gods are not invented, they are discovered
             and rediscovered!
(Though Christianity was once a fierce fanatical madness
             destroying gods and temples.)

See how the Egyptians made pictures speak . . .
a true language, saying we did this
               like this, would catch fish
          row, hunt fowl, lead cattle,
                         carry goods,
                            like this, like this!

But Egyptian gods are dead
             and Greek gods are living still.

Venus, the love that ennobles the body.
Apollo in the breathing stone.

They now exist in modern Paris,
                city of barmen and bistros,
of bateaux mouches and métro—
                     so soon to be extinguished.
Seen for a moment, like a carnival of fireworks,
        to 'Ohs' and 'Ahs' of surprise,
                            the glittering appearances,

they vanish, leaving some paintings—
"Paris as Seen by the Masters",
poems, or music,
caught in the amber of art
like dead flies, with twigs and leaves around them.

Sure it is good to be living. But we don't
really matter that much. The permanent matters.
Something that art reveals.

There are no short-cuts to it. Time
is the main highroad to eternity.

The tender vanishing life,
evanescent shadows playing
over the gay straw hats, young faces—
as the French Impressionists captured life on the wing.

From the High Renaissance to the nineteenth century
painting adjusted its forms
(beginning with myth and divinity)
until it had found the actual, real,
in the immediate moment of living.

But a moment is brief.

And no sooner had they found it
than the mystery vanished in formal vision,
a spray of lights, or a cloud of shadows,
or just paint flashing across a screen.

Now they are far away and more remote than ever
from the sensual present.
And they have gone to the secret processes
of nature,
that makes form, out of whirling chaos, and energy,
the place of the unborn, titanic powers.

What we want in art, as in life, is the numinous present.
Gods, a secular Apollo.
Aphrodite.

She says that desire can be noble.
But they have hated desire, and have destroyed beauty,
so that no one was there to tell them
desire can be noble.
And therefore desire became ignoble.

Now that we want to believe in desire,
we say, "Venus is desire . . .
Venus is the goddess of love."
But Venus is not the goddess of love.
Venus is the divinity of desire,
and nothing is more hateful to her than ignoble lust.

"Desire can be noble," she says.
And that is why it is not easy
to honour or to worship Venus
(no more than any other divinity),
for she would have you improve your character,
and every virtue,
so that even chastity is sometimes part of her ritual.

From PART III

2

Have you seen the weeping beech
hanging like a green pavilion?
Or the tulip tree
reaching up to heaven?

Have you seen the cedar?
The kakee tree, the gingko, the lobed sassafras
—have you inhaled their fragrance?

The glistening leaf of the strong oak, suber,
the slender white birch,
the dappled maple,
the tough sticky pine, swelling with rosin?
Have you sat on the moss among the brown cones?
Have you seen the contours of the leaves?
Or listened to the silence in their shadows,
or the rush in high winds?

I have gone to the green pavilion of morning
and watched the dahlia open her eye.
I have seen the violets breathe in the blue light
under pendent leaves.

There's a delicate beauty of India, in a ballroom dress,
and a handsome negro, to whom all about are loving and
friendly.

There are the lovers, it is night.
By the stairs he is kissing her mouth, and she clings.

A girl practicing the violin at her window
gives me the glad eye and a groaning note.

The paradox is that pride, which is self-seeking,
results in the most impersonal and enduring monuments,
the great houses, and arts.

Poets like rooks follow the plow.

Mostly, people are obliged to be human
by a certain amount of insecurity and fear.
To be just to the weak is the great test,
like doing good without a reward.

As for Auschwitz and the other horrors
        it's not so much that the victims were Jews
but that they were human.

It has concerned the Jews too much
                and the Christians too little.

"Look after things . . .
        and turn that slave girl into cash."
(Rufus to Epillicus, 100 A.D. in Britain.)

Surrounded by sword hilts and helmets.

Utillam puellam ad nummum redigas / and the diary of
                                        Ann Frank.
"Make sure that the warheads are ready—"
                        top secret (2000 years later).

Even in the highest cultures, mystic India,
        there was wanton cruelty.

Though Assyrian and Egyptian gods
                        reek of power,
Greek gods were delicate, vulnerable—
        their gentleness and gracefulness
                a harmonious union of the elements.

"Begin by loving earthly things," says Plato,
        "for the sake of the absolute loveliness . . ."

Despite all the blood of the innocent
the leaves glistened
as the still-trembling bodies fell into the earth.

About your murders nature doesn't care
        because death is not such a bad thing to her—
just a more rapid turnover.

God is a great gambler, always counting the winnings.

He never counts the chips that are gone
only the ones he's raking in,
millions that weren't there in the beginning.

All right, all right, everything perishes.
But what a pity to fold up the particulars
and yield to others!
Over and over! The same over and over!
The particulars must go, and we are particulars;
and will never again be, no, never again be.

Does today regret yesterday?
Now we are today, yesterday, and tomorrow.
But who is there who is all yesterdays and all tomorrows?

For whom all days and every day, forever, is today.

How could there not be?
If there would not be, nothing would be.
Is there a line without a surface?

If all are moving, is not something still?

They say that nothing is still.
And they say there is no surface.
Then nothing is real. It is all fiction.

But even a fiction's for someone to imagine.
We imagine a small part of it, for a small time.
Who is there who imagines all of it, for all time?

Genocide is not a new thing,
we exterminated the North American Indian.
The English killed off the Britons . .
There are no Neanderthal men!

Think of the more general condition of nature,
it will save you from hysteria
and prepare you for the textbook facts.

Man is a new thing. Indifferent slaughter
was there from the beginning.
We have only begun to care.

A short History of Massacres could be prepared
in a week or two of research:
China, Assyria, Egypt, Greece and Rome,

the "Story" of Carthage, of Thebes,
of Peru, Mexico,
Japan.

Perhaps we have now begun to care.

The Chinese are preparing to exterminate us.
No wonder.
Or maybe the Negroes will finish off the whites. Surprised?
It isn't pretty but it's natural.
We're only slowly learning to care.

In fact, pity seems to be a recent idea of God's.
Who knows?
Maybe it's the new order he's trying to bring in.
(He sent "His Son".)
Don't despair. The real wonder is that any pity is there!
How simple things would be if there never were.

Two thousand years?
You can't think of history in terms of weeks.

Monkeys will watch a rhinoceros die
without batting an eye.
How childlike the animals are!
The pet monkey, the dog.
As though evolution itself were a growing up.

Can we imagine the adulthood of us all?
The gods within us, aching to be real.

Maybe they have their world
        but they want us to equal them in this one.
We must help. Act as envoys.
We have their seal and authority.

That's the wise thrush
hopping about on the newly watered ground.
Ti-ti-ti-ti-ti-ti! (six steps and a pause)
                Listen.
Peck! Ti-ti-ti-ti-ti-ti! Nothing.
Then nip! a worm!
The wriggling thing fell out on a leaf.
                The bird turned away.
Leave it? No chance. Back to the worm
    —doomed thing! He gave it a good shake.
Threw it. Picked it up. Mangled it. Jabbed.
Then flew away with the bit in his beak.

From the point of view of the worm
                it was all unforeseen.
Exit into a new world, of light, of air.
                The end!

How could anybody grieve? There will be other worms.
                "Feed my birds."

From the point of view of the bird
            something that happens every day:
"One of my favorite worms."
                Very good.

It was all well arranged. Till we began to mourn.
Memory. And love. And a wish to save,
                snared us.
So that we wanted it all as permanent
        as remembered things.

Memory, our first replica of the unchanging,
an imperfect piece of eternity.
It is a co-existence. Refusal to forget.
A first realization of death
(for death is only change).
Now that we have memory, now that we mourn,
how can we accept death?
Yet how can we be so foolish as to avoid change?

We live divided. Sometimes not very happy.
Those who remember more
think most of other worlds.
Those who love, mourn.

Let us take what we have and not desire more.

The short eternity of art, of love.
We are not gods,
nor lucky beasts.

Someday, in the great future, perhaps
there will be men
no longer torn,
for whom time is one eternal now
and change an ever-unchanging change,
who see the permanent in the impermanent
and the same rose in every dying rose.

We have memory to will the future,
love to enjoy,
visions of perfection that we might improve.

Like a lens our thoughts focus the light
too near . . . too far
or midway between the distant and the actual
where, on the rock, the minerals gleam.

Look: "Still Life With Chip Frier"
(every mixed-up goddam thing in the kitchen).
How about cutting a couple of holes
in a couple of poles—
"The Hollow Women"?

Everything that passes is semblance for a day—
the dirty Thames (dirtiest of rivers)
with all that it bears—
and the few of us look back through time
seeing the Titians, churches, the Roman shields
and catch for a moment a glimpse of pattern
—O not the real, not substance
but a hint of sequence—
that others, caught in time,
pitched from moment to moment, falling,
may find an instruction, a hope,
a breath of encouragement . . .
But how could they cease
their watery progress to listen, to think of the emptiness
that still surrounds us, the shreds of our meaning,
in the precipitate rush of existence?

. . . A time for the artist to relax,
a time for simple truth.
To come back to the simple fact,
to humanize his art.

Ah, Wyndham!
Cophetua may still rhapsodize
but at the Tate
I did not find Ezra, where he used to hang
almost life-size.

The beard replaces the necktie,
the pub gives way to the espresso bar.

And poetry is the fruit of experience!
The present is always present!
Ha! Ha!
All you've got to do is be there to enjoy it.

The dead don't care—they're neither here nor there.
Something keeps the world always full,
like a daily newspaper.
An atomic ticker-tape?

Ghost writers?
In a corner of a London museum
I saw the ballet shoes and feather-white dress of Pavlova
in which she danced The Swan,

with old clothes, torn gloves, and bits of broken glass
from those times.

And Adelina Patti's tiara—
a triumph in La Sonnambula—
buried in a downstairs room.

Eliot's Waste Land, which we thought "the age",
is not England,
not even London,
but his own Lower Thames, down from the Bank,
that he knew so well.

If Eliot had been the young man carbuncular . . .

I said, there should be an increase in beauty
since there are more women than men
(only the beautiful will propagate their kind)
But then, what about ugly men?
Maybe we could take turns . . .
Anyhow, hyacinth girls are somewhat rare.

Even a common beauty, on Trafalgar Square,
might please a tourist
with camera notebook in mid-air.

Thalia, ripeness is all . . .

I passed the house in Ebury street
where Mozart wrote his First Symphony.
People who have lived in these streets,
in this world . . .
And went to visit John Stuart Mill, Carlyle.

The perfect life is possible:
ducks in St. James' Pond
have it as good as could be, the state of nature
under the protection of man.
We cannot provide this for ourselves?

Man seems to be against nature from the beginning—
naked, he cannot live
without taking some animal's hide or building a sloppy den.
Must make it "artificial" before he can survive . . .

And then there is so much choice,
between a cave and a castle wall!

His job's to create a new nature that will imitate nature.

Society is a work of art—as haphazard,
you might say, as this one.
It is an order, of a new kind.

And speaking of art, what could be more beautiful
than a couple in their sixties,
pudgy, wrinkled, with hands like brown claws,
walking down the path together, arm around shoulder,
talking of intimate things?

Or is it nature? They say that marriage
is against nature.
Wanton promiscuity . . . men getting their teeth smashed,
killed over a woman . . .

Someone invented marriage.
It's certainly a work of art—
                    that "imitates nature"!

There are pools of reality—the galaxies, the seas,
                    the domesticities.
Snow's world and Farrell's. Or this today,
                                        and Elizabethan London.

While Russell talks about "dry rain".

I once wrote to Ezra, "If they explain your poem
                they'll kill it."
He answered, "Don't worry. They won't."

Ilex Aquifolium, the pale-fringed holly.
The Strelitzia like a tropical bird,
            the hanging lamp of the purple fuchsia.
The rose Spiraea and the royal lily.
(And birds come to eat from your hand—
                    would you want to harm them?)

Gleditschia   Dietes   Regal Lily

Not that the poem doesn't have a meaning.
                It's what holds the thing together,
an invisible ghost.

I have seen the parts of a flower
                floating, detached from the stem,
yet knowing somehow what to do.
Growing, drinking in rain.

Callamandra   Zantedeschia   Gloriosa

And an orange tree, with dozens of fruits

You would know from their love of flowers and birds
                the English are a gentle people.

The lady told me she turned her garden into a sanctuary
and couldn't paint the eaves,
there were so many nests.

(Though last night I saw a man in a state of passion
that was like a fury from another world.)

There are plants that choke their kind.
Lilium Burbankii, tiger lily . . .

(This business of Hitlerism was like that,
a trans-human fury,
like the heat of galaxies, incomprehensible to us.)

Even around a coffee table
someone will break out in tears.
'To agathon, the good' is a flower of the temperate zones.

The fruit of the Magnolia of Yunnan
opening their great pods
and the Cashmere Cyprus of Tibet
that hangs like drapery, green and brown.

Nymphaea and tropical fish

But the rhododendrons were not in flower.
"The rhododendrons were not in flower!"
"Ah, you must come back another time."

To see the famous roses
Mme. Butterfly, Sutter's Gold, Masquerade,
Christopher Stone, Misty Morn.

(Was it Mandeville wrote—
"How Roses First Came Into the World"?)

Primula Japonica . . .

Ah, Waste Land!

3.

"What's the answer?" students often ask.
From happy childhood to miserable old age—
what's the answer?
A kind of exploration.

Though young crocodiles feed on insects, older ones eat men.
When man arrives the wild animals are always threatened
with extinction.

The new god
DEOXYRIBONUCLEIC ACID
(Deus, ecce deus)
When you consider the complexity of organisms
all our worries are nothing but a little surface trouble.

The rhino horn is made of compressed hairs.

Each particular life—the whole universe.
I heard a naturalist say: "Men and animals
cannot live side by side."
Where man is, nature is soon likely to become barren.

The point was made that man has survived
because the big cats don't like his meat.

We are separate universes,
cut off from the others.
"I love you because of your absence."

The porcelain beauty of English women
has been the ruin of English art.
Or maybe art shapes the women.
(To love one would be 'a storm in a teacup'.)

Beauty by artistic selection.
"To love her is a liberal education . . ." wrote Defoe
of a certain Mrs. Hastings.

The next stage in evolution?
Nature is working on it.
A stomach that will digest Fish & Chips.

Cf. Harmsworth—
"The public press is the concentration of all that
is best in thought . . ."

And Charles Lamb: "I love the very smoke of London . . .
The man must have a rare recipe for melancholy
who can be dull in Fleet-street."

But the smoke has thickened
(mixed with car gas)
and Fleet Street, today, would make him melancholy
without a recipe.

We need a smoke-proof lung possibly?
("I made it out of a mouthful of car-exhaust.")
Perhaps the oil reserves will not last.
Only the women remain beautiful.

It's something you contain, or something that contains you.

But there are no consolations in Sigmund Freud.

Henry Moore's people, out of Dali,
and the desert ossifications of the Surrealists
may be prophetic.
Against which you have the complacency of the pipe-smoker
and the man with the Reader's Digest.

The average income in Britain is $1000 a year,
but in Burma it's about 40 (forty dollars).
World population 3 billion,
annual increase 50 million (roughly the population of Britain).

Conventional dullness, RSBA.
Yet maybe the architects are the only modern artists,

making their structures of light and efficiency—
for the clean new life, of activity,
honesty, openness to fact;
but we'd have to bring the whole world into it.

Yaws must be eliminated. Fewer people but happier.

There is so much incredible suffering
that crucified Jesus makes one laugh
at his comfortable nails.

Pity is just a beginning.

We've bitten it off, we've got to chew.
Take biology: "The Biological Basis of Human Freedom."
Or look at the birds.
They're very small characters that say everything
(God's little aviators).
And all the man-fearing animals.

As Canaletto painted an eternal daylight
over his Regatta on the Grand Canal;
or that foreverness in the eyes
of "A Family Group" by Lotto.

Eternal chicken, eternal bread and fruit . . .

The great place of art
is halfway between this world and some other:
Hals to Hogarth, Giotto to Botticelli—
including the English pantheon, Aristocracy.
But the unknown will remain unknown.

This is our gift, to extricate joy
from earthly things,
what is distilled of transcendence
out of the visible.

With Riemann, & Einstein,
with Hoogstraaten's peep-show,

and Vermeer, the fascination of symbolism.

A heap of straw, in which a needle of truth lies hidden,
Turner's "Evening Star"
over the sea . . .

The greenery of many mounting trees,
with nary a cloud, a spot of light
held in the memory.

Against pessimism
la vie a connu le froid et la mort
dès le commencement.

Success counts. What else matters?
The courage of the creation against the cold.

When that is over, quiet submission, and sleep.
If we retain our identity in the afterlife,
who among us will remember that he was Caesar?
If we remember this in another
how could we not be unhappy?
I only love what I know.
Even what I know vanishes. How could it be otherwise?

Do you want to abstract the birds from the trees?
Or will you preserve all the leaves?

A few great men in the museums,
like the keystones of London Bridge
or the ruins of Coventry.

Yet all that ever was is, there is only one present.
And time is the breathing spirit, the movement
by which it speaks.

The deer walks on tip-toe.
The seal was once a cat.

What is the zygomatic arch?
What is the condyloid process?

Consider the dugong and the manatee
that feed on aquatic plants.
Or the giraffe, eating the tops of acacia trees.

There are animals you wouldn't want to meet, still in Europe,
the wildcat of Scotland,
the wild boar, the wolf in Portugal, the lynx in Sweden.

How much of it all do you want?
How much can you take?

Will man be the gardener of the world
and bring order to Eden?

Perhaps the price is too great—
and there is 'the will to suffer'.

Perhaps the price is always to suffer!

Perhaps it is not possible . . . perhaps love is not possible . . .

But I am satisfied. Rest awhile
on the cushion of time, here and now,
and prepare, for whatever it is it gives.

I said to my friend, "Don't read this,
it'll make you dizzy."
But she read on, said she couldn't stop.
"What is it?"
I said: "The vertigo of freedom."

A living thing asks itself
what milliards of years no plant, bird, or animal . . .
It was never part of their business.

Why stop at all, she said, why not go on?

In nature, beauty is a case of and/or.
There are still the atoms, and the stars
(and all the crude machines made by man).

"Of course I can't stop," I said.

Nature is interested in beauty, look
at the excess of the peacock.
It likes to try the extremes, of smallness, of size—
all possibilities.

Nature is a lot like man, it goes to excess.

The little children in purple jackets
with tiny raincoats over their arms
march in the sunlight to the park.

On the grass they divest, and dance in their tunics
Ring-a-Rosie, and Go-in-&-out-the-window
while the teacher sits close by.

So they get an education
in the ways of nature, and are nature.

Nothing is ever finished.
Hokusai, Hiroshige, Kuniyoshi
(lightning like Japanese script)
and the Wm. Morris Co.

Modern artifacts, our Danish knives,
lace, Wedgwood, china—
even a poet or two on the boards.
Jazz.

"Electronic music should go with poems."
"I'd like to try a harp and a drum."
"An outdoor auditorium
with music tunneled underground."

"How about syphoning sea-water onto the moon?"

Somewhere in there I see a gleam
like the sun in the leaves,
a great, bright, fearful, beautiful bird.

Where will you find it?
Like God, the sun does not intend to be seen.

Imagine all things at last explained!
Finished.
Packed in the brain . . .

What do you think we're up to?
What do you think this is?

Crumbs to feed the birds. A little curiosity
helpful for finding a roost.

Some of the element in which we live,
like islands in a sea of possibility.
A burning glass that warms us
and sharpens the distant sun.

I look at these people.
Never again to see them.

The young, and the old with their small last pleasures,
sitting in restaurants or working in shops—
they will be gone.

This voyage is almost over. I think
how everything will go on here
as before. As it must. And yet I know
that somehow I am a part of it, in it
for good—or I do not live at all.

Not an individuality but an identity,
is what we really are.
That continues, as it lives in the body,
in fraternity with things and men.

It is the whole reality that is always there;
something that we are, that we become,
                    that now we cannot know or share.

This is all new to me.

The half of a moon.
The sound of feet.

Should I ask that tree?
              Listen with my ear to the ground?
Study a flower for a sign?

I will take it all in and wait
                          until like a Univac
I suddenly throw up the sum.

This will be always true, as it is now (as all we do),
and each living thing an enameled bird
                                                    of paradise.

There were sixty people at the High Mass in Southwark
                          lost in the great vault,
their prayers drowned by the Underground.

I looked for the past in the present
              (in the Borough streets placards were out
                                       for "Othello" and "The Merchant"
                             right by the precincts of The Globe)

And the bank by the Thames where we walked
                        (in the 'dry rain')

I saw a graveyard where the stones had been ranged
                      along the side as a low wall,
while the space itself was turned into a children's playground.
We are always trampling on the bones of the dead.

T

It all comes down to this life of ours
of which you have the pieces
right in your hands.

EPILOGUE

In the daylight of departure from the shores of light,

the sea was a white burning cloud all afternoon.

Locks hanging over the counterpane
or grapes spilling
out of the bright horn.

"Light."

Only in the reflection of portholes
gulls
flash across mirror, a dumb sequence.

The sea as an escritoire.
That pale blue
and violet
heaven.

Like dreams before they begin, a tunnel
at the end of which a blue grotto,
silently set with shrubs, shines.

Silence, in the glass light of so much meaning
it looks like indifference, and purpose so large
the details are left to chance.

What I think when I am alone

of the sea, the road of adventure
—what the soul sees between two lives. Hearing
only
the plaintive seagull's infant cry.

All the animals are eccentric,
therefore we are affectionate to them
and amused.

Too much of one thing, human.

To die, to drown, to be free
of everything human.
A clean new beginning, a ghostly embryo.

Whispers, on the burning crystal—of things to come.

In this world, everything is immortal,
it merely changes.
A new form, of the same old thing!

That manifests itself in change, even in incompleteness.

Naked bodies lie on the deck, new girls,
perfect limbs,
shoulders,
crotch.
Clean to love.

(Sir Kenneth says a small body
is easiest to love . . .)

Also, tall rhythmic bodies
that look sensitive to touch.
There is the soft, sweet female, of any shape,
and the secret inward parts
of their genesis . .

The body, embryo of love. A bare beginning.

New bodies. Cherubs.
The promise of shapes to come.
Embryos of men.

No land. It is all a wild turbulence
of possibilities.
A spiral nebula. A sea of milk.

We go into darkness, into deeper darkness,
where all embryos are shattered.

An emptiness, void of meaning,
a signless nil
cancelling out all mathematics.

The great zero of nature, in which the little numbers flicker
like a halftone of nazi crosses
without significance.

Concentration camp of souls.

With gas chambers and crematoria:
"genocide" of all mankind and all animal species.

"All these must die"—by order
of the Supreme Authority.

A scientific experiment.

Yet "eternal not-being and eternal being are the same"—
though the ship's report says "a confused swell".

Under the sea, as over the sea,
the weather is almost permanent.
We have escaped from land-made weather.

We have escaped from great old buildings,
from new cities, from car exhaust,
from English gardens, Rue de l'Opéra and Via Veneto—

into the grey indifference where nothing stands,
where only the sea moves,
that is itself nothing, and everything.

Hush. It beckons. A secret void.

And the wild pulsations . . . listen . . .

(I do not want the blackness of the sea
            only such knowledge as this foam, the mind, creates)
Speak to me . . .

Nothing, heavy as lead.
I saw the night like a dark fury spreading its wings
                        to hide the day,
under feathers of cloud black as mourning.

The dark rushing horizon seemed to flee
            to the north and south from the sunset
where the light turned, twisting, broken and grey—
            white foam, frozen feathers.

You whispered to me and leaned in the darkness
                        to hide from the evil,
saying, "Take me away, save me . . ."
and touched my knees, while the black water
                        swirled around us.

We must go.

Where the bios shapes the body, as we shape our dreams
                        out of memory,
into the image we need.

Look at the lineaments,
what are the parts of any woman that please?

Someone you love, or have loved, or will love.

A mixture, that makes things new
            out of dissimilars, making a third.

Limbo. Amorphous cloud. Alembic of nature.

(Why work in mines, said the miner, in London,
            when I can stay in the open air?)

There, somewhere, at the horizon
you cannot tell the sea from the sky,
where the white cloud glimmers,

the only reality, in a sea of unreality,

out of that cloud come palaces, and domes,
and marble capitals,
and carvings of ivory and gold—
Atlantis
shines invisible, in that eternal cloud.

An architecture of contradictions and inexorable chances
reconciled at last,
in a single body.

The iceberg came toward us,
like a piece of eternity,
like a carved silent coffin, out of the night,
and stood in the shattering sea,
serenely still,
and disdainful, while we looked with awe
at its still beauty assaulted
that knew neither time nor change.

In darkness. Infinite night.

Fierce, all-devouring night,
featureless, fearful night.
Sweet, all-dissolving night.

O love. O new bright love.

There is a drop of snow on death's car.
A cloud against the dark mountain.
The white of the moon.

There—is reality. A white flame.

I see my angel, flying over the water,
to the blue that's like a thin gas flame around the world.

Leave me, I said,
            spirit that must rise above today and tomorrow.

Already I hear
            the creatures are laughing at my words.
No one understands. It does not interest them.

Even my anecdotes must fail.

Fragments of poetry that float on the water
                  as common seaweed.
A bottle. A board.

How will I separate them
                        from the drift of snow?
Or amanita, from the edible food?

"Poetry is meditation."

("For the masked ball," said the professor,
                  "you should get dressed up as Buddha.")

But no one meditates.

An unfair advantage.
                  The brain has an unfair advantage
over the creatures.

We have more than we can use.

One of nature's excesses.

So that these exercises exhaust the average mind.

Learn to be more practical, simple and kind.

Nothing—is always true.
In any crisis, it's the best thing to do.
Nothing—is what it comes to.
It's where we begin.
Nothing—is what we like to do.

Everything comes of nothing.
It "never faileth",
it is as good as charity—those who have nothing
also have faith and hope.

Nothing is silent. Nothing is simple.
Nothing is left to chance!
Nothing is at the heart of mathematics,
and number the nothing in all that is.

We come to land by a pleasant shore:
to roads, houses, people
we have not seen a long time,
so that our dreams must be corrected by the familiar still.

Talking, gladly, of the long journey ahead.
And all the future.
It's always a new beginning.
The real, or the unreal—
beginning where you are.

We meet many travellers
who report on the way
of hidden beauty, joy, or honour
in the four corners
of the lost continent.

There is the sea. It is real.

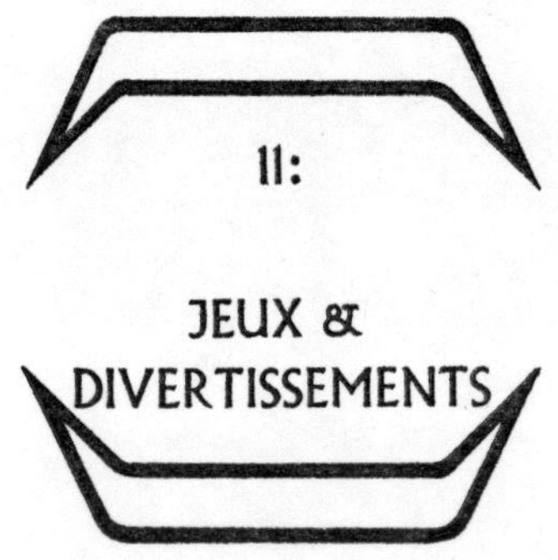

11: JEUX & DIVERTISSEMENTS

ALBA

O Aphrodite
look down on the clover face of youth
                torn with desire
look at the lonely middle-aged
                without satisfaction
look at the old in their flannels
                denied and played out. . .

Give every man a gentle responsive lover
            —and if more, a child of his own.

EROTIC TROPES

Attacks of satyriasis, true love, or religion
come more frequently with age:
            we are done with small passions,
now it's all or nothing (as it must be), so
                        let it be all . . . .

I am mad for your body, I am mad for your soul
            (even God is mixed up in this)
He makes his animals queerly—
a tiny fish that *lives* in its mate's vagina,
                    and a giant who wants to.

As if one could do nothing but make love.
Yet that's how we'd like it, really:
            no answer to life's awful mystery
but an inexhaustible yearning for the one thing—
                        cunny and lingam.

One theory has it that after forty
          sex can no longer be satisfied, it can only be aroused.
You have those "corpuscles of Krauze" frozen at acme. Agh!
          Like a door that will not close:
the reason's plain, it's the hanged man's erection.

However, the young will say they have it too.
          And it's no relief to be underage.
That way, it's true, we escape "the monster" . . .
          Though now, only in your arms I forget the fury.

Only in your arms I am pacified,
          holding you in a lasting embrace
Anything less intense than an orgasm gives me *ennui*.
Stay that way!

At my age, the 'outside world' has little enough to offer,
                    a few sexless bricks
of gold some new silver spoons. . .
(still, if I don't get out I'll die here too).

What I mean is, all life's a religion
                         that withers away,
and this one, which inspires the others, is all there is in the end.
Or before the end. Of course, at the very end
               there's still the serene senile look.

Actually, because it is everything it isn't everything.
          You realize it's only one solid goddam thing—
                                        like a knot in wood.
But not the whole wood.
It just won't go through the vacuum grid of extinction
                              and rattles like a skull in tin.

Darling, this doesn't mean I don't love you. I think of nothing
but you
—but somewhat desperately!
Quality counts. That's why it hurts
to make it quantity.
Forget the cause, look at the effect of this.

It matters, that we older lovers fail you,
by giving too much or not enough.
We know the truth, but can no longer live by it.
And it doesn't mean a thing, really.

We do not believe that much in the one gift we pray for.
Trust in my little faith
and sense of order, now that it's over—

a poem about sex, not against sex,
and not for it either—
just giving it, despite the fuss, a bit of proportion.

LES RÉPÉTITIONS

I

Again Violetta's dying.
One would have thought once was enough.

When art becomes that real
who wants it to be repeated?

And yet we do.
(it's nice to have that first kiss again.)
In fact, nothing is much worth repeating—
even the sex we vary
as we do.

"Let's go to the movies."
"Another cookie?"

The mystical experience is another thing.
Like art, it's something that should have happened
and therefore we repeat it.

(We are never bored
with something that should have happened.)

"Let's do it again, maybe this time
it will happen."

We repeat everything, looking for art.

II

What you give some men never get
not in a lifetime of looking—
the difference
between sex and no sex
is that between your speaking body
and any other woman.

'Did you find art?' she said. . .

If anything was that perfect
we'd repeat it because it was perfect
just as we repeat what isn't
because it isn't.

THE PROCESS

If nature could have managed it
it would have made it all unconscious
like digestion the working of glands or a reflex action—

some in fact do go blotto
when it happens
"a peristaltic movement" you hardly notice
in your higher centers

(leave it to the highest of all
the dark entelechy that made us)

But we have to meet and communicate
before we can begin
to be simple and perfect as a natural process,
that is also as mysterious as any—
like peristalsis, glands, or a hand closing.

FICTIONS, SUPREME OR OTHERWISE

Making it, we do not fret
whether the man-made heaven is the real heaven;

forget, for once, that the heaven we make
is all the heaven we'll ever get.

CONFIDENTIAL

One day
you gave me such a bang
with your long neck
and ponytail
dear girl
that now six years later
I still think of your
qualifications
as I write this letter to the Dean
of Graduate Studies

SAD THOUGHTS

If you are like the others,
        eat hamburgers & onions
with "Pepsi-Cola," dance the zack-zook—
you do not find perfection.

And if you're different,
        stop on the *grey light*,
                eat escargot parfait—
you too are lonely.

BUT AREN'T ALL POETS POETS' POETS?

"Writing to please myself," as Marianne Moore put it
                    once in Brooklyn;
now on the blackboard, forty years later,
                                        and out of her hearing.
Or "I join these words
            for four people"—
circulation 5 million by 1960.

Don't try too hard,
                    saintly virgins—
you may crack the world's eardrum!

FROM THE CHINESE

As the breeze rose (I guess there was a breeze)
the maple dropped its catkins with a rustle:
        I saw an explosion of pollen in the air.

In the morning light the leaves shone
        light green, like a lamp in the back yard.

BRIGHTNESS

It is like love, this vision
taking us away from nonsense
                    into a great silence.

Youth is over
            joystick, bicycle, the prowess of the body:
I would have it again, but more
                  I would have it all erased
for some radiant future—

something it all contains and that contains it
like apples in autumn we have not eaten.

FRAGMENTS[1]

Ah yes, ah yes—the pieces!
Your broken pipe, John . . . and the remnants of a dinner.
Only God is whole (like a work of art),
                      and the greatest metaphor—
man enlarged to take in heaven,
                      complete and perfect.
We are fragments torn off from creation,
and our poems fragments.
Therefore we find only pieces, and leave only pieces.

FRAGMENTS[2]

We fools made our poems
as fast as feathers of snow
and the winds took the torn flowers. . . .

Nothing remains

The dry plains remember summer
and golden sunsets
over back yards

Cats, clatter, and the tin horns
of yesterday

The children's hour that is no more,
like the wind, like the snow.

ICE CREAM

That strange energetic impulse . . . .
Be glad you did it.
A thousand poems that no one considers good:
These were your vices, delicious ices—
"Gelati! Gelati!"

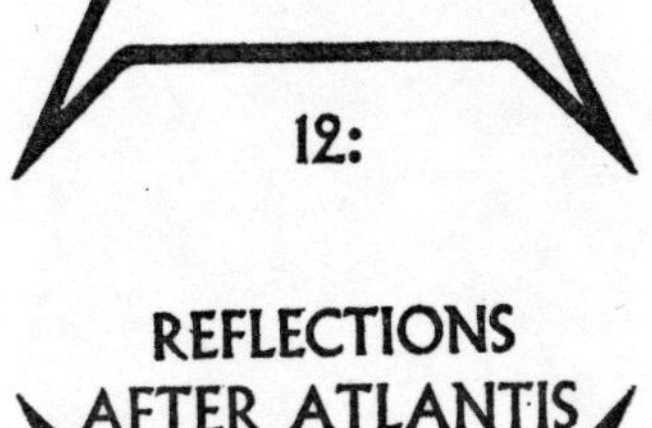

12: REFLECTIONS AFTER ATLANTIS

THE DEMOLITIONS
(For John Glassco)

I

The biggest name in Montreal these days is Teperman.
It stands a yard high, in front of old buildings:

TEPERMAN Demolition

Teperman is working hard. I've seen the remains
of old dilapidated lovely city sections
                    go down in rubble—
"No Parking" signs over the lot.
And the whole city, including Cathedrals,
skyscrapers, the statue of Burns,
                    and our three universities,
level like these lots, as they will be . . .

Teperman works fast. What does he care
whether any building we want to stand
                    for eternity goes?

His business is DEMOLITION
                    and swinging metal balls.

II

The block on Stanley (I've got to check with the street post)
where our bohemia was just commencing
                    and the beatnik gallery burned
where Leonard had his rooms (offered in friendship
                    to MM CD and others)

where the Riviera coffee house and the tenements and
Betty's "Tailor"
had their domicile
where Sutherland set up the First Statement
and we read the poem by Souster, in manuscript,
"The Groundhog"
and Madame No-wee-jee-ess-ka carried on . . .

So picturesque
so picaresque
so European

Like the ruins of Warsaw, our only Latin Quarter
has been razed to the ground

I look at the empty space, and think of all the Hungarians
locked out in the world. . . .

III

The new buildings that rise on the rubble
in flocks, to the langorous clouds,
will stand all night in their stories of light
swinging a searchlight to fear

but will not remember the slums
at the roots of their bones
nor the dead who went down on a Stryker frame
nor the unfledged young
who disappear.

Lonely for new glory they wait
for long leaseholds and the penthouse dwellers,
their corridors filled with maidens
too simple to love, and too ignorant to care.

CANADA: INTERIM REPORT

It's a wilderness
      between the jungle and the sea.

Empty. Waiting for "culture".

Jokers like jackpine across her middle:
the blowhorn epic scenery
            of Heavysege and Mair,
or flatlands pioneered by the Scotts
(or the beast poet, or the needlepoint muse).

Nowhere a great love, nothing good. The English are dying
      at home—read Compton-Burnett, Amis, Wilson.
How can they flourish, here?

A wilderness of Poles, Doukhobors, Ugrians, Letts & Goths
Hammer-headed Umbrians and Welsh bruggs.
      They crowd the hills, read their own weeklies
            filled with mad politics and bad poetry.
Queer religions thrive: crude epics of the people.
Angry young men *shave*, to be different.
All the women have flat feet.

This wilderness is full of stones!
We are not affectionate.

Q: Are there whales in Hudson Bay?
(If there aren't any now, there never will be.)

Stop pretending: "Central Hardware"—at the edge of town.

And newspapers "for whom books do not exist":
The Weekly *Albertan*.

The Sun Dance of the Plains Indians
taught them what *they* must bear.

All those proud animals
    that wandered over the hills and plains,
the bighorn, the bison, the caribou
                                        and the Indians
whose faces have an equal grandeur—
                                compare them with ours
whose heads, mounted, would disgrace and shame
all conquerors of the world.

(Sometimes I think life is much too serious
to be fooling around with mere literature.)

Honesty!
Mit Tränen in Augen I saw the bead-work
                                of Canadian Indians—
a first poor attempt at beauty!
And the "burial moccasins" for a baby
                            with pretty beads underfoot
(to walk in the Isles of the Blest).

But now, in the great unoccupied country
            (cows like fleas in the distance)
they multiply on the Chinese counting-frame of the hills.
Make an emptiness, or an industrial mess.

(Where man is, nature becomes barren.)

The settled stone-age dwellers
                                have replaced the Indian
(uniform rectangles, with lids, in the suburbs).
But the country, the vast unoccupied country—
        to see it! even as tourists!
                                From Percé to Banff
mountains, plains, lakes—and the human wilderness
                that fills them . . .

If men from Mars came here we'd make a poor showing.
However, Nigerians travel and look for investors
    Canadians, to develop *them*!
What can you do

with rocks, prairies, rivers
    just below the timber line,
but grow jack-pine, erect grain elevators?

"No monuments, no Elgin marbles."

We're trying to make a living.
The warbling vireo has outdone our elegance.
The Eskimo's our only real artist.

We need Nigerians to develop *us*.

"Someday there will be cities in the Shickshocks."
(But I am living now!)
A wilderness, between the jungle and the sea.

A man with the face of Stephen Leacock is all I could find.
Or hefty little western girls like young cow hands
with hale Ukrainian cheeks.

We have our breeds: our Oriental West, where the East is West
        (really an English nook),
and Middle Canada, from Middle Europe,
and the French—and Scotsmen everywhere.

I guess we need half-breeds, mixtures
                —more Indians, where none remain.

(Duncan did his best
    but it was not good enough.)
We poets try to fill in, as the noble savage—
in fact hardly noble at all.
Chief Crowfoot had it all over us.
        (Shot, while refusing arrest.)

The Red River cart, for them,
    was a step forward in industrial design.
Now Massey-Ferguson tractors carry on
        (fine examples of stone-age art)
with Don Messer's Jubilee.

In time, art becomes more conscious,
till even the lack of it is possible.
Mind you, we're coming along
(Mr. Jones ate, how many airline dinners?)
too fast.
"See Canada—on foot!"

Or like Purdy, ride the rails.
The underdog's view is all we have:
Realism
of proletarian poets.
And, on the other hand, English decadence.

Dachyma Cocos or Tockahoe,
a fungus, mistaken for pemmican—
called "Indian Bread".

"Dead Souls" that we are.
Maybe a revolution will save us.
But I have no "secret solution".

The CPR caters for a non-existent First Class.
"They are *not* different from us;"
but "They have more money."

Says Walton: "Read Jenness
on THE INDIANS OF CANADA."
(He sent me the book, kind soul.)

Voltaire said it: "The Canadian savage persists."

And a Beat poet: "Quebec, what a horrible city!"

"Went to the University of Montreal," wrote Masters,
"learned nothing and returned home."

We take a beating, not only from ourselves.
What is it
that we're "such second-rate sons of bitches"?

(Mediocrity, said Anderson,
—the Canadian identity.)

Others have their pride; we have our inferiority.
Wind-swept Estevan, Regina, Saskatoon.

O CANADA

Who owns Canada? You know who owns Canada
to the extent of 16,000,000,000 cash
(How much do you think the place is worth?)
increasing at the rate of one billion a year—
perishable imports
paid for with natural resources.

By the time we reach One World
we'll already have been one Continent.
There are short-cuts to the future.

Brighten the corner where you are!
At the desperate bookstore everything was going at half-price.
And on Scarth Street I found
CANADA DRUG & BOOK
Co. Ltd.

And the yak:
"Just because it's a book,
do I have to read it?"

Seven thousand years of history
—and look at where we are.
O brighten the corner.

It's mankind, not merely Canada,
has a long way to go:
an undeveloped planet.

With several million years
                of pre-history.
We haven't done un-well
    considering what
we had to start with.

Look at the world like dazed farmers,
    hoping hail will not fall.

What do you expect poor man to do?
        Walk on his head?

Layton when he dined with Everson
    felt he had "betrayed his class";
I, in this restaurant, try to think
        this is where we all belong.
Give us time!
        (First Class, where there is no class.)

The gnarled common people
feel the cold wind of the woods
blow on their grim hands.

Read "Save Yourself" where it says Serve Yourself.

A wilderness is the land gone wild.
The thing we do not have
                will come easy
after the grubby soil has been raked.
Do you think luxury is so hard to enjoy?

What else is poetry,
    when it comes down to fact,
but an *excess*—of words?

Displayed with economy!

WILL BUILD ON THIS
VALUABLE CORNER
TO SUIT TENANT
Apply Max Goldman
CANADIAN JUNK CO. LTD.

Without ambiguity, such as
SHAPE OF THE EAR-
TH. By Patrick Lynch (Mac-
millan Co. of Canada Ltd.)
$2.75

The shape of words.

They are banging with hammers across the street.
Tzack! tsach! takk!

So the businessman has replaced the warrior and the aristocrat.
(Air Edition of the Globe and Mail,
its ten financial pages.)
As those who do most good, they eat well.

"He's a real pusher."
"Buy him out"
"I don't know"
"It's a necessity"

"What d'you figure we ought to allow?"
"Well, their part sales
dropped off about a hundred thousand dollars this year."
"Did you get the copy of my report?"

"I don't think we'll have too much trouble
picking up that 100 thousand."

Buy art—is that the problem?

A list of 'library books' in the Leader-Post.
(How I believe in the book!
That it should perdure . . .
                                        and grow
and that we be there:
the artist somewhere in the middle.)

But he must change his function,
      practically, adjust his lines to it,
like the men of power.
As the businessman has replaced the warrior.

A new use for artistic vigor.

Ah, wilderness!
What we owe to the Indians—
            "a poor utilitarian culture"

cranberries	tomatoes
vanilla	peanuts
maple sugar	sunflowers
green peppers	corn on the cob
squash	wild rice
pumpkins	lima beans
avocado	cocoa and chocolate

A lot more than wampum. In a pinch, they ate pemmican,
      Indian salami.

As for artists, there are forty-five whooping cranes
      left in the world (April, 1962).
But the last two failed to breed.

The toughest men who ever lived
have become old, and weak,
until they couldn't take it any longer,
                                        and they died.

All this is much too serious, for mere literature.

Dying is mainly "passing the buck"
                                        i.e. the torch.

O God, O Canada.
We'll study our progress with an adding machine
    —counting the great dead.

So it's by dying that we're increasing,
adding to the heap of glorious discards,
                              as the poor grow richer.

Nothing matters to the chimaera, but change.
Not even the Paradise of Might-have-beens.

Whatever it is, never satisfies.

Onward!

The dirty atomic cumulus we leave behind.
(Our Defence spending has been cut 86 million
                by austerity.)
A horrible wet summer, a fall in credit.

But "survival" is not in danger
        for whooping cranes in the least.
We are the gardeners of the world
in Eden yet to be.
Why else have we understood the boundaries?
And conquered to make love?

Like the lady who stole a seat from the speechless immigrant
and became kind—with shame!
(He had given her the place, out of courtesy, the fool.)

Grab, with decency.
Magnanimity
        is for those who have grabbed enough.

So man will learn to be generous.

As for us, we're at least semi-developed.
We can begin to be big.

The Human Empire—pax humana—
our national concern.

Look, sunset on Lake Superior,
a slick of white cloud
over amber-glowing water.

The dark forests, of birch and fir,
and sky, silver above the roar
of the train.

Pioneers, O pioneers!
(they're all dying at 96
with mortgages in arrears)
You see what a mess we've made of it,
as the end of "Canada's Century" nears.

Silence trips up the tongue.

The new poets will find a better technique?

Hey, rocky emptiness!
Vancouver lights!
Slag heaps of Sudbury, for miles and miles . . .

(Nature becomes barren—
or is it a new fertility?)

"Wolfe's the North's Greatest Bookstore"
and "Campus Boys' Wear"
where there is no campus.

Ah, trees, homes, and fields.
(Culture is money, give it a little time.)
Morning, a new day breaking.

Overhead the jet-planes trickle.
Children chirp and cheep.

That's all the world there ever is or has been;
    the rest is a dimension.
"Look for it in your solar calendar."

Everything, whatever it is, is a kind of Canada.

A CIRCLE TOUR OF THE ROCKIES

Even the chance relations
      of mountains to one another
blue against blue, are a kind of form.
I only make it by being where I am.

The jagged ones, also, a play of irrational forces
      as, at rock bottom, they say it all is—
but only to emerge, like an island, green out of chaos.

The purpose of disorder
      is to clear the slate for something new.

Think of mountains as an obstruction,
                  Les Rocheuses of the mind.
It is all crowded there
            beautifully;
but beauty is a glut on the world.

Geophysically speaking, a magma
(orchids are likely to get crushed,
            many a tender thing).

And you get some of those sky-rocketing constructions
            or boulder-strewn barrows
                  and thin glacial streams.

Clear it to the peneplane of un-being,
            an empty consciousness, space-time, a blank page,
and something begins again. God knows
maybe just a new area of suffering. Of experience.

For whom?
      This, for us, it happens to be.

A mountain of balsam, fir, spruce, avalanching moraine and clay
      (mountains are top-heavy, always falling down),
like the universe, wearing itself away.

The frightful devastation of a forest fire
seen eight years later,
like a cemetery, a battlefield, a Belsen of unfilleted bones,
may serve for an example.
(One doesn't like to see whole universes going up in combustion.
Put out that match!)
But it happens; in fact constantly.

There's a whole mountain like a flat empty wall
waiting for decoration.
Your mind—could become that wall.

Or sometimes you get a stand of skinny trees
that simply gotta go.
It's the heights and depths, in the hollow of vastness,
for which it all exists.

Some of this, you don't know whether people have built it up
or the forces of nature,
architectural theatres, stairs of erosion, strata.

The canyon of Nature
yawns to an infinite nowhere multiplying on destruction.

To cup an Okanagan
folded somewhere in the belly of deformation.
It must be so desired! At least when had,
a superhuman satisfaction—
to us! who are merely human!

(Don't forget we invented that thing;
but to think of it is to prove its existence—
you can't merely 'conceive' that your life exists.)

The first mode is non-existence,
out of which, by some twist of necessity, a world
of superabundance comes.
Once they start it they can't stop
piling mountains on one another,
rearing and eroding, until there's this—

an unpredictable satisfaction, like a girl to love.
It could have been some other, but it was something
    you always had in mind.

It looks like a stone-quarry in some of these parts,
    as in strict definition it is.
The utility of nature, for man, is unquestionable;
but as in art, we are always asking: 'Is it a good in itself?'
It is. Anything that is good for anything
    is 'a good in itself'.

It has reality, for which, in the end,
    everything must have come to be.

Some of these things must be believed to be seen.
Though for that matter, we all see enough.
The thing is to work back.

Some people, you can give them the Rocky Mountains
and they want something. Unsatisfied.

Evenings, the deckle-edged hills help us:
certainly as something good, that speaks for itself.

And in the morning
the wave-movement of the hills
    like that wave-theory of matter
where fruit-trees flower in their folds
as the right wave-lengths gather in the Good.

I have believed that the whole universe is speech,
        a communication.
That speaks for itself. And wants to be believed
        to be seen.

Very useful, too, for us, who like to have something to stand on.

The mesocosmos
    in which we spend our lives.
Mack, Mike, Mess—the three worlds.

At least one thing in the Bible is true,
man is the first gardener.
Last night I read Genesis to Gregory,
'a bedtime story'—
He created this He created that
(he didn't ask who).

'Enough?'
'No, read me more of that one.'
Like the red book about Zeus, Neptune, and Venus:
the twice-told tale.

G—(Geological process) created all the mountains,
the meaningful generations of matter.
Mountain begat stream begat field begat orchard.
The Bible of science.
(Both, of course, equally absurd.)
But useful, to the Bomb makers and to children
at bedtime,
therefore real.

God is a brand-name for things
that come out of the chance factory—
French beans, 'Made by God'.
Christ—God, Inc.

Look. A sweet cunt of meanders
meeting on the hill.
Nature is playful.

And people come to the mountains
for mere pleasure.
Turn it into a cheap resort.
The world
as entertainment, is no good in itself.

All kinds of amusement
and in the end we go into the Fraser Canyon
(just before dark).

What an experience!
And that is why God etc. . . .

The Crucifixion according to one theory.
Eternal return, another.

Everything; there are even flatlands in the Rockies, swamp soil
and crushed ice in purling streams.

Real pleasure is a very gentle
occasional thing.
You don't go after it. Let it come.

And it's good sometimes to get that feeling
of the world looming over you suspended in space—
precipices, cliffs, and precarious ascents
before the mind can come to rest.

Let it extend, as it does.
It's something that just goes on.
Somewhere, everything happens.

We live in the most-possible-of-the-best of worlds.

Also of the worst, per contra.
That's the chance one takes.

But the worst is a desolation
somewhere outside our ken.
What we can bear to suffer,
or enjoy, is limited
by what can do some good,
that has already emerged, as a kind of valley, or garden
out of the void.

Clearly, the rest is up to us
—whether there is 'meaning' or no 'meaning'
(the atheist and Methodist agree).

There are tones in that infinite landscape
intuitive of things to be.

But mostly the parched mountains, and poverty.
Ranch life, poor soil, sadness peering out of sunburnt eyes.
The skinny unhappy child and the mother
in a cotton Sunday dress.

A poor universe, even if the best
possible.

Hot, dry, hemmed in by the mountains
that no one can traverse really,
slag heaps of unscalable rubble,
a cosmological waste
leading nowhere.
You live here, trapped by their sloping sides
and steep rushing streams,
a provincial in the great world—
small, stunted, alone.

Are we concerned with small pleasures
because the great are closed?
Prevented by mountains from seeing the scale of mountains,
we stay on a stable-land or a plain.

The church itself is a hulk
hiding the light of day,
and received knowledge, our science,
a glittering wall.

But the mountains are beyond conception,
like the whole cosmos, that naturally is
unknown, inscrutable, incredible—

that we're stuck with—
the immense sum of nothingness,
and the ecstasy of it all!

As if to say: 'Yes, at last! It is this I wanted!'
'Yes, we are here—to see!'

But then, in the end, we sleep
(withdrawn from circulation)
and the world goes on, building and dismembering its mountains:
the great small enterprise where we have a ticket
for only one ride—
The Circle Tour.

Sad, when the merry-go-round stops.

Thank you.
It was exhausting, but impressive.
We lost our topcoats, of flesh and animal skin.

If there is anything we can remember
It was the silence
in the great canyon of extinction,
and the loud invisible accord of things that live.

Violet last shadows of evening
on the high cliffs.
Darkness is in the current, reflective colours.
In the mountains, even the dusk is brief,
for sunset, over the peaks, comes early.
And the strenuous life takes its toll.

Then the cooler trees, cedar and fir, in the hollows,
damp, dark,
thoughtful.

Turn away from it all.
What is it?

A circular movement of matter,
swirling, atomic salt.
Distant, the dark trees, the snow patches,
turbulence of waters
indistinct in the night—

a glimmer, a dot, lost
somewhere in the void

where everything good is possible.

CONTINUATION I
(An Infinite Poem in Progress)

So let's continue

These vast accumulations
          not without reason, that may have a use
or none

'Putting together lyrics'

With sex, talk, contact
between eating and excreting,
a process you do not need to understand

And the stratifications of silence
as Wayson S Choy put it,
               the mute affirmations of space

Beyond a few select sentences, in our lives, there is nothing

What did you expect,
          the poem to write itself?
               or to start a hurricane?

Not really, only a language
to contain the essentials that matter, in all the flux of illusion

Pebbles, that shine through the cobbled grey
                    that emerge, in time's liquid flow
as diaphanous heaven

And the viscosity of things
How it all hangs together
          hiding whatever it is it hides

The real world
is silent, we must be silent to hear it

Like the mind making poems
hid in the texture of language

An ecstasy after an ecstasy
to the quiet mind
        (whenever you pause)

The censorship has been thwarted
After long silence
"Yes, I wanted to if I slept ten hours. . . ."
What did you dream of, dragons?
                        (a broken marriage)
or happiness?

Follow the arbitrary virtues
And like a good engineer of troubles
                        try to put it straight

A lonely sparrow sits on the backyard tree,
                        a brown leaf that will not fall

Materials, lumber, gravel, nails
wherever men are working, trucking, hauling, alive

There's the embittered flood

My morning coffee has cost some labour
to peons in Brazil, to stevedores lifting bales
And what have I done to deserve praise?

(For some have achieved while others suffer)

Lenin like Jesus
        teaches what most men forget
No system but a moral fact

As silly Willie found
(wanting real sex, after 'Byzantium')
the forms of things 'eternal' are taken from the things of time

What's going on in that stupid little head of yours?
'The delightful aroma of excrement'

Of horses or people, equally good
            (God likes it)
God became a worm, and lives in faeces

A philosophical theorbo, this body and spirit game

Who cares, does anybody care
about your precious mind and what goes on in it?

'The Eliot papers'!
At Harvard University they have scholars who can, who do,
            make use of these things

He dwelt among us
I saw him with my own eyes (put your finger here)

But to accumulate lines, is not that a pleasure?
To weave them into patterns,
                        is not that happiness?

(Parody, dear Ezra, a loving imitation
you once called it criticism)

O the poet that incredible madman
        possessed by what he hardly knows or comprehends
See him coming toward you, his fat cheeks on fire
convinced of his potency, his craft, his supreme art
that no one needs or understands

One of God's handymen
for whom the future is still the word, hot out of chaos
and the present cracked mirrors, in which his own face
appears and reappears on every wall

He is possessed with possibility,
            will create the world anew

until it burns out, or gives place to others
just as hot and new

Sometimes his models become real and part of nature—
even for me and you

Accumulate, accumulate!

These industrial wastes, and the land we live in
(an orchard here and there)
A swish of snow across the landscape as a train passes
(or is it our own vapour)
with objectivity so hard to attain, and yet who wants it?
We put our pieties on paper

It's what you think when you don't read that is your own
Keep your thoughts commuting
even on Sunday

As the automated society
is more and more given over to pleasure
it may well be
the one day left us
for a little work

For an audience of one, because the popular
reeks of paranoia

Still trying to find that meaning which eludes us,
to extricate why the molecule prances

There's nothing wrong with God that a little atheism won't cure

Let's face it, he became overbearing
Then came the Messianic complex
And in his rage took to burning people and torturing

So we sent him to the white hospital

Now he's out, quite humble   Oecumenical
Under our tender care he may live at home
There is even hope he will make sense again someday

All good poems
          are conversations with God
and there is never any hurry
                              to publish

He doesn't mind, as any father
            would rather be less gifted
to find more gift in his son

Humility

You know, Eliot put quotations around lines we might recognize
I put some around a few
I thought too good as coming from me

All this backstairs wit
                    I've never said it

Also the possibility
that I might have said some things twice
The poem? It takes a lot of courage
          to run a household, more to run a nation
What of the universe?

(My dear
I want no harm to anyone, have no enemies
And for myself ask only one thing
                              your happiness)

Grains of sultry silence
grind in the eye . . .

The conscious mind knows nothing of art
That's why we forget our dreams

(Give a dying man a post-hypnotic suggestion
see if it works . . .)

It's come about so that anyone
who isn't killing himself for pleasure
is a puritan

Poets have become unamiable, untamable
innumerable, unnameable

Having lost the dream, I feel no anguish
Lassitude itself is a dream

Still a happiness between the thighs, an awakening
A pleasure in the morning light

The human ecstasies, on which we bank
drifting slowly toward oblivion

This first edition of 3,000 copies, printed by W. & G. Baird Ltd., established in Belfast since 1861, was printed in Northern Ireland. The text is set in 11/12 Baskerville, with section headings in 12 pt. Albertus. Printed on Clan Bulkrite. Cover and book design by Glen Siebrasse. Of this edition, 100 numbered copies are signed by the author.